MW00674487

# ARTIFICIAL INTELLIGENCE VERSUS GOD

# ARTIFICIAL INTELLIGENCE VERSUS GOD

Published by Voice of Evangelism Ministries
P. O. Box 3595
Cleveland TN 37320
423.478.3456
www.perrystone.org

This book or parts thereof may not be reproduced in any form, stored in a retrieval system, or transmitted in any form by any means—electronic, mechanical, photocopy, recording, Internet, or otherwise—without prior written permission of the publisher, except as provided by United States of America copyright law.

Unmarked Scripture quotations are from the
King James Version of the Bible.

Scripture quotations marked NKJV are from the New Kings James Version of the Bible. Copyright © 1979, 1980, 1982 by Thomas Nelson, Inc., publishers. Used by permission.

First Edition © 2023

Printed in the United States of America

ISBN: 978-0-9895618-3-9

All rights reserved

Cover Design/Illustration & Layout: Michael Dutton

# CONTENTS

## CHAPTER 1

# A Two-Thousand-Year-Old Warning

The pursuit for limitless knowledge. Eradication of disease. A quest for eternal life. Digital immortality. Unraveling the mysteries of the universe. Creating gods. Becoming God.

Suppression of information. Revision of truth. Surveillance of citizens. Reduction of populations. Manipulation of DNA. The merging of man and machine. Empowerment of elitists. Enslavement of the rest.

Welcome to the Ancient World, reengineered.

Two thousand years ago, Jesus gave a warning about the time of the end. The phrase, "the time of the end," alludes to global events predicted in Scripture, all of which will begin to occur around the same time and with increasing intensity. Biblical signs of the end will serve as indicators that trigger the return of the Messiah.

What is one principal sign that the world has entered the time of the end? In Christ's Olivet discourse in Matthew 24, He gave the same warning four times. He mentioned wars, famines, pestilences, and earthquakes in verse seven; however, He clearly emphasized and warned His followers to beware of the possibility of being *deceived* (Matt. 24:4, 5, 11, 24).

The Greek word for deceive is *planao*, meaning, "to lead astray, cause to wander, cause to stray from the path or from the truth." It is the same Greek word that Paul used when he warned of seducing spirits leading people astray at the time of the end (1 Tim. 4:1).

In a biblical context, the primary warnings have been interpreted to refer to deception through false prophets or false teachings. However, a manmade threat has emerged that has the potential to thrust the world into a global deception that would permanently and negatively impact information gathering, decision making, politics, and nearly every other area of our lives. It could alter humanity by creating an environment of delusion that would become impossible for the average person to detect, at least until it's too late.

Billions of dollars are being invested globally into systems of technology that are designed to turn machines into humans and humans into machines. As you will see, people once again are attempting to build a Tower of Babel where nothing will be impossible for them. They desire to become like God. This goal will be achieved, they believe, through AI, an acronym for artificial intelligence.

Artificial intelligence is described by those in the world of technology as the science of leveraging computers and machines to mimic the problem-solving and decision-making capabilities of the human mind. It simulates human intelligence and can go even beyond that. At its simplest form, artificial intelligence combines computer science and massive amounts of stored data to solve problems that ordinarily would be solved by humans. The AI system uses these databases to access information for machine learning and deep learning. AI exceeds the speed of a human's abilities as it attempts to make predictions and provide knowledge, information, and advice based on everything it collected from the database.[1]

Examples of artificial intelligence with which we already are familiar include:

- Siri, which responds to questions it is asked;

- virtual customer service agents that have replaced online humans;
- the global positioning system (GPS) that has replaced hardcopy maps;
- computer vision, which recognizes images viewed or tasks performed on a smartphone or computer, and then uses that information to make recommendations based on perceived interests (such as items you're shopping for, websites you visit, videos you watch, and so forth).

Two types of artificial intelligence are narrow (weak) AI and strong AI. Narrow AI performs a specific task, such as answering questions based on user input. Strong AI can perform multiple functions and eventually teach itself to solve new problems. Machine learning models require human intervention, while deep learning models try to imitate the human brain. Deep learning models are designed to handle complex problems. Self-driving cars, chatbots, and virtual customer service agents use the deep learning model, although it's obvious they still have a lot to learn. The theory of artificial superintelligence has also emerged.

AI experts tell us that strong artificial intelligence surpasses the ability of the human brain in many ways, such as its ability to process information over 100,000 times faster than a human brain. Developers have discovered that AI accesses available data and unexpectedly teaches itself new skills without being prompted by human designers. Developers have been surprised to see this, and they say it's mysterious.

Experts warn that, within a few years, artificial intelligence is expected to gradually replace eighty percent of the jobs now being performed by humans. During the month of May 2023, nearly four thousand jobs in the United States were replaced by artificial intelligence. This is just the crack in the door. Investment bank Goldman Sachs predicted that AI could eventually replace three hundred million full-time jobs globally and affect nearly one-fifth of employment.[2]

Projections indicate that artificial intelligence will eventually replace human journalists, writers, authors, and newscasters. It will replace people ranging from fast food employees and agriculture workers to those in administrative, legal, and medical professions—even surgeons. AI creators downplay potential job losses, claiming that the AI industry will generate plenty of new jobs. They claim that the AI market will generate $1.3 trillion in sales and advertising spending for the technology industry. It seems clear that the primary goal of innovators and investors is the gain of money and power, even at the expense of humanity.

## THE STRANGE WORLD OF CHATBOTS

Job losses are one problem, but that isn't where the potential deception lies. The deception lies in the information being created, the value system of the people creating and inputting the information, and the ability of the machine to read, compile, and draw conclusions correctly and ethically. Let's look at an example.

Recently we witnessed the release of an artificial intelligence system called ChatGPT, which has already enamored many who have experimented with it. ChatGPT was started by a company called OpenAI. The company writes on their website: "We've trained a model called ChatGPT which interacts in a conversational way. The dialogue format makes it possible for ChatGPT to answer follow-up questions, admit its mistakes, challenge incorrect premises, and reject inappropriate requests." It also states that you can "get instant answers, find creative inspiration, and learn something new." Open AI admits there are limitations on ChatGPT, including that it "sometimes writes plausible sounding but incorrect or nonsensical answers. Fixing this issue is challenging."[3]

One question or command fed into a computer or smartphone allows the artificial intelligence system to research and write a response to your inquiry. The system will quickly research millions of pieces of information available online, then give you an answer, all within an astonishingly short time span. College students are already utilizing this to write their papers. Businesses are using it to write snippets of programming code. Ministers are using it to write their Sunday sermons. People are creating artwork by giving the application basic commands. Recently, someone asked ChatGPT how AI is linked to the Second Coming of Christ. The answer it gave was that it can cause great deception.

Even though ChatGPT sometimes answers correctly, developers have warned that there is no guarantee all the answers it presents will be correct. The system has been known to "hallucinate" and fabricate lies about people, which has resulted in threats of lawsuits, once the victims figure out what or whom they should sue.

Here are recent examples. Brian Hood, a mayor in an area northwest of Melbourne, Australia, is threatening to sue OpenAI's ChatGPT for falsely reporting that he is guilty of a foreign bribery scandal. Jonathan Turley, a law professor at George Washington University, was notified that a bot is spreading false information that he was accused of sexual harassment that stemmed from a class trip to Alaska. The bot didn't even correctly name his faculty university, but that isn't the worst mistake. ChatGPT quoted an article from the Washington Post, but no such article even existed, and none was ever written.[4]

Law professors say it's possible that ChatGPT could face defamation lawsuits over the persistent creation of false information. The first ever defamation lawsuit against OpenAI was filed in June of 2023 by Mark Walters, a radio host in the state of Georgia. ChatGPT created a bogus story that Walters had defrauded and embezzled funds from the Second Amendment Foundation. Every statement made in the ChatGPT summary was false.[5]

Google developed a chatbot called Bard AI that they asked eighty thousand of its employees to test before it was released. Reviews were terrible, with one employee calling the bot a pathological liar. Another said it was cringeworthy, while yet another employee said the bot gave potentially life-threatening advice on how to land a plane and how to scuba dive. Bard AI was called worse than useless, and employees asked the company not to launch it. Google launched it, anyway, adding disclaimers and calling it an experiment.[6]

Large companies such as Samsung, JP Morgan, Chase, Amazon, and Verizon have banned staff from using generative AI applications like ChatGPT at work because they do not want company data to be leaked. Once uploaded, the data that has been entered into third-party applications is stored on external servers and could ultimately be disclosed to other users.[7]

There is a great likelihood that artificial intelligence chatbots will continue to provide false information, since the information it accesses is only as good as the data sources from which it gleans. Would chatbot developers intentionally create a database of false information? Or could the system become corrupt all by itself?

Consider that in 2023, we learned that Silicon Valley tech giants, at the request of our own government, censored information to make it unavailable to the public. Dissenting commentary was removed or slapped with a false information label. Anybody who merely questioned the approved narrative was censored or banned and accused of spreading harmful information. The Constitutional right to freedom of speech was thrown out the window, as only certain information was approved for public consumption, even when that information was knowingly and blatantly false. Purveyors of fake news controlled the news by calling the truth "fake news."

A conservative group that rolled out a free speech web browser called TUSK used OpenAI's ChatGPT to create an AI chatbot called

GIPPR, naming it after Ronald Reagan's nickname. Open AI shut it down because the group refused to conform to their requirements for what can and cannot be said. TUSK's CEO said, "The GIPPR bot had been modified to not be highly biased in favor of a leftist agenda, something which seems to be of critical importance to the original creators of ChatGPT."[8]

What will happen when the public becomes dependent on artificial intelligence to answer questions, conduct their research, and write their papers, articles and sermons, but the only sources of information from which AI gleans will be fake news, weaponized propaganda, and corrupt data? Eventually, the public will become dependent on artificial intelligence to do their work for them, because we have proven that we are addicted to technology that demotivates us the more we use it. Too many people already have a problem discerning truth from lies, so one can only imagine the nightmare scenarios this will create.

How will we know that the information being created by artificial intelligence is accurate and true? Will the content be slanted? If conservative content is banned, then we must assume that AI is accessing only leftist and controlled content. Humans program artificial intelligence, which means that the content creation depends on the people doing the programming and inputting the data. If conservative content and truth are removed, where does that leave us?

The objective of developers is to convince people to trust AI and the content it creates. Tech giants want people to believe the machine is intelligent; therefore, it must be dispensing the truth. They won't want the public to suspect that con artists and propagandists are behind the creation of the content.

## HOW IS THIS WORKING SO FAR?

It has not taken long to prove the point of false information and deception. In July 2023, it was reported that ChatGPT performed worse on certain functions than it had in March of 2023. Its performance was checked in four areas: solving math problems, answering sensitive questions, generating software code, and reasoning visually. Researchers found wild fluctuations which are called "drift." These drifts can lead to vastly different outcomes, according to Stanford computer science professor James Zuo. In March, a number could be identified by ChatGPT as a prime number 97.6% of the time. By June, the same number was correctly identified as a prime number 2.4% of the time.[9]

Scientists at Rice and Stanford Universities found that feeding AI-generated content (called synthetic content) to AI models drives the model MAD—an acronym for "Model Autophagy Disorder." As people use this technology, and the technology generates synthetic content for the user, that AI-generated synthetic content is added to the database of human-generated content. Remember, human-generated content is supposed to be the foundation of AI.[10]

When AI combs through the data to provide the answers and material the user requested, it is now recognizing both human and AI-generated data. Before long, this causes the output quality to erode. ChatGPT is already being used by corporations and individuals to generate content, yet even before the database was corrupted by synthetic content, the answers the system generated were not always correct. Now the bot seems to be going haywire.

To make matters worse, Google and Microsoft have already embedded AI into their search services. Here we have a form of artificial intelligence that was just introduced to the public, and already it's lying to us.

## SMARTER THAN HUMANS?

It is difficult to imagine that something artificial could be better than the real thing. My wife collects artificial food, and while it looks appealing on the table as a decoration, try eating a cake made of cardboard, clay, and plaster and convincing us of how good it is.

We are told that artificial intelligence will become smarter than humans, and that it already surpasses humans in many ways. Let's assume that machines will indeed become smarter than humans, simply because the machine can access and process unlimited information so quickly. How will humans compete? Once people are forced to become "as smart as machines" or else be thrust back into the Stone Age, what will people do?

One option will be chip implants. Technology developers want to create chips or brain implants that will boost the brain and give us intelligence superpowers. The implanted individual will have the knowledge without ever having to study or read the material, thus becoming a walking computer of information. Already we see the time coming when it won't be necessary to spend tens or hundreds of thousands of dollars for a university education.

Being discussed as well is the likelihood of uploading your entire brain, including your thoughts, feelings, and memories, onto a computer. Imagine, humans programming machines to become more like humans, and humans uploading their brains to become more like a machine. It sounds like dystopian fiction, but proponents believe it is *necessary* to merge man and machine. In a bizarre manner of reasoning, they even believe this will defy death.

Klaus Schwab is chairman of the World Economic Forum, a globalist organization whose members push for global governance and other ideology most of the world's citizens would oppose, such as radical climate change measures, absolute control of the global population, and the merging of man and machine. Klaus Schwab speaks of a global revolution that he calls the "Fourth Industrial Revolution." He believes that this revolution is fundamentally different from any previous revolutions. This one is characterized by "a range of new technologies that are fusing the physical, digital and biological worlds, impacting all disciplines, economies and industries, and even challenging ideas about what it means to be human."[11]

Schwab believes that this revolution of technology will change, not what we are doing, but what we are and who we are as humans; it will change *us* by merging us with the digital world and machines. "The very idea of 'human' being some sort of natural concept is really going to change. Our bodies will be so high tech, we won't be able to distinguish between what's natural and what's artificial. Inside our own heads is the most complex arrangement of matter in the known universe. You might ask yourself: Can we get to be superhumans?"[12]

Whenever new technology is introduced, it is typically the younger generation that accepts it right away. They will have no problem engaging with artificial intelligence because of all the perceived benefits, despite job losses, false information, and innovators' warnings that artificial intelligence could overtake its creators and control mankind, or even start a worldwide nuclear war. Unless they realize the threats and heed the warnings, it seems plausible that the enticement of new technology will make possible a great spiritual defection from truth.

End-time deception will be enhanced when AI creates false biblical interpretations or promotes teachings contrary to the Bible. With the ability of AI to produce fake news, false information, fake pictures, and fake audios and videos, we can clearly see how this will be used to deceive entire populations. Deception will go mainstream, and once it reaches a certain point, there will be no turning back and no ability for humans to stop it. Some innovators of AI warn that, once a line is crossed, artificial intelligence will be impossible for humans to control.

The further artificial intelligence advances, the more information we will have at our fingertips. The more information we have, the more useless information we will have, the more propaganda we will have, and the less likely people will be to know the difference. How much information and knowledge do we need? How much is too much, especially when people are no longer able to discern the difference between truth, lies, deception, and propaganda?

Facts and fiction, truth and lies, it all travels at the same speed across the World Wide Web. Once posted on the internet, something can go viral within an hour and take on a life of its own. The information could be smoke and mirrors, propaganda, or half fiction being presented as fact. Great illusions create great deceptions.

There are dangerous potholes and steep, rocky cliffs along the information highway. In this book, we will see how tainted sources and the blurring of truth will corrupt the AI information highway. Many in the media and government are already masters of this process. Even throwing out the word "alleged" or claiming "anonymous sources" is enough to protect dishonest journalists from liability.

We are being set up for a massive flood of emerging technologies that will change every aspect of life. We will examine that information from biblical, historical, and current sources to show that the strange prediction in Revelation 13:11-18 about the kingdom of the beast is now becoming possible.

## CHAPTER 2

# SCAMMERS, LIARS, AND A CRISIS OF FALSE IMAGES

In 2014 in Tenerife, Spain, a zoo was performing a drill to ensure they have a plan if a gorilla escapes. A veterinarian, not knowing it was a drill, shot the gorilla with a tranquilizer before learning that the gorilla was not a gorilla, but a human in a gorilla costume who was part of the drill. Later, the zoo reported that a veterinarian had shot one of their staff by mistake during an escape drill, but that the employee was not wearing a gorilla costume or pretending to be a gorilla.

The first story made more sense. It was mistaken identity—a man in a gorilla costume. The second story, the media correction, made no sense. A veterinarian shows up at the zoo and shoots animal tranquilizer into a man. How does someone mistake a human dressed like a human for an escaped gorilla?

## BEST FRIEND DEAD?

My routine after I get ready for work in the morning is to eat eggs and an avocado, drink coffee, and go to the office where I turn on two laptop computers. One is exclusively for writing books and messages, and the other is for internet research. One morning when I turned on the internet laptop and saw the news, I was in shock. The headlines read that the night before, my close friend Jentezen Franklin had been killed in a car wreck on his way to preach. The report detailed the accident and said the police were investigating, and even told how the church was reacting.

I told my wife to call Jentezen's wife immediately and get details. I was devastated as I sat thinking about how the Lord had given him plans for the future, and wondering why He allowed Jentezen to die without fulfilling those promises.

It took an hour to finally hear back. Jentezen's wife reported, "He's not dead or hurt or injured. He's alive and well. That's a false report!"

Later Jentezen called me and was shocked when he read the article, which by now was already circulating in a few online news magazines. It was all a hoax and a lie.

## A CASE OF MISTAKEN IDENTITY

Being alive while seeing your death announced in the news is bad enough. But being a victim of mistaken identity or intentional lies can destroy someone's life and reputation. Men have been arrested, charged with a crime, and incarcerated for years, only to later be released when new DNA evidence proved them innocent.

I have been the victim of mistaken identity on a few occasions. The most dramatic case for me was years ago when a woman contacted our office by e-mail, saying that an unknown man had been emailing her pictures of himself. After showing her friends the pictures, she was informed the photos looked like a man named Perry Stone. The woman was irate to think that a married minster was sending her pictures.

Neither I nor any of our staff knew this woman. Furthermore, I do not have (and never have had) a personal email account. The office staff receives all emails for me because they come through the general ministry email account, and the staff will respond on my behalf when necessary. My wife Pam contacted this woman and asked her to send the pictures.

The woman sent the three pictures. Some of the office staff looked at them and were shocked. The guy could almost have passed for my twin. The differences were our eye color, teeth, and eyebrows. The real kicker was that the guy was drinking wine, and I abstain from all alcohol. When these things were pointed out to the woman, she apologized. Her friend had seen me on television and "just knew it was Perry Stone."

Perhaps the man simply sent his pictures to the wrong email address. Or, considering what we know about online scammers, this might have been someone trying to defraud this woman.

## THE SCAM OF CATFISHING

Scammers pour through millions of photos on the internet, then use a collection of pictures from accounts of unsuspecting men and women to operate their scams known as catfishing. Scammers set up fake social media accounts with the stolen images, then contact men and women, often older people who are divorced or widowed, through their social media accounts. This is all under the pretense of developing an online relationship that will allegedly lead to marriage. Their purpose, however, is not romance, but to scam a lonely and unsuspecting individual out of money. They use all kinds of fabricated personal stories to prey on people's emotions and obtain money.

These romance scammers are generally located somewhere overseas, especially in Africa or other countries where they are not likely to be caught and prosecuted. Everything about them is fake—fake pictures, fake social media accounts, fake resumes, and a laundry list of lies to go along with it. The scammer will message his victim to say that he was on his way to the airport to visit you (after purchasing a plane ticket with the money you sent), but he is forever delayed because of a stolen passport or a mugging that landed him in the hospital. Sometimes he steps off the curb and gets run over by a bus. Until next time, please send more money. After all, he *really* needs it now that he's laid up in a body cast from this tragic accident.

YouTube is full of sad stories of both women and men who wired thousands of dollars to these scammers. They were roped into cashing in retirement accounts and taking out second mortgages on a home that was paid for, all because they believed in a scammer's false promise of love and marriage.

Other scams that typically originate in countries overseas involve phone calls, emails, or text messages in which the person being contacted is tricked by a false story into giving passwords or personal bank account or credit card information. Millions of dollars have been emptied out of bank accounts, all accomplished within hours through electronic deception.

Twenty years ago, scammers used fax machines or email accounts to send letters from a crook who claimed to be a wealthy woman living overseas who was left with tens of millions of dollars after the sudden death of her husband in a car accident. The widowed woman wants *you* to have most of this money because she doesn't need it. All you must do is wire her $5,000 in good faith, along with your bank account information so she can make a deposit to your personal account. These fraud attempts acquired the name "Nigerian scams" because that is where many of them were said to have originated.

As we have witnessed, with each new leap in technology, crooks and scammers waste no time figuring out how to use it for their own personal gain. As we also have witnessed, people are easily deceived by scammers and liars.

## DEEPFAKES

Another deceptive aspect of AI is its ability to create fake pictures, videos, and audios of people, thus potentially placing them in falsified compromising positions. These videos already have a name: deepfakes. These deepfakes can place a person with anyone at any place, when in fact the people might have never met one another, or never been in that location.

The danger of a deepfake is the ability to use a computer application to falsify information with the intent to change the public's opinion of the person or organization. Deepfakes have been released on social media, where they have tricked millions of people. Some well-known individuals have had to legally defend their reputation by exposing fake and false information that was created by someone who used the means of artificial intelligence. Even the FBI has issued warnings about deepfake videos or audios created with artificial intelligence.

Sometimes the user takes existing source content and swaps the actual person for another person. They also create entirely original content where someone is doing or saying something that they did not do or say. The deceiver only needs a short clip of your voice to create an entire audio of you saying something you did not say.

Deepfake technology has been used to create political satire, and people have been tricked into believing it's real. A discerning person can tell when something isn't quite right about the video or audio, while knowledge and common sense will tell you when something is off about the content itself. However, in some instances, the content seemed so real that many people were deceived. Deepfakes are predicted to become the most dangerous form of fraud that has ever existed.

In 2023, a woman received a phone call from an unknown number that she almost didn't answer. But since her daughter was out of town on a ski trip, she wanted to make sure nothing was wrong, so she answered the call.

On the other end of the line, she heard her daughter's voice sobbing and saying, "Mom! I messed up!" The Scottsdale, Arizona resident said that the voice she heard over the phone was a dead ringer for her daughter.

Then she heard a man's voice call her daughter by name and tell her to put her head back down and lie down. He demanded a million dollars for the daughter's return. He told the mother that, if she called the police or anybody else, he was going to pop her daughter full of drugs, rape her, and drop her off in Mexico. In the background she could hear her daughter crying and pleading for her mom to help her.

The mother happened to be at a studio where other women were present, and they made phone calls to confirm that the daughter was, in fact, safe and in her hotel room. Her daughter had never said anything that was heard on the recording, nor had she been kidnapped.

This is voice-cloning technology, and it needs just three seconds of your voice to come close to creating an audio that sounds like you. A large enough sample, which according to experts is just twenty seconds of you talking, is enough for the technology to clone your voice inflection and emotion.

The troubling aspect of the phone call in Arizona is that the daughter doesn't have social media accounts. But she had done a few public interviews for sports at school, and that is possibly where the caller picked up her voice sample.[13]

The FBI warns that, if your voice and your information are public, you risk allowing yourself to be a deepfake victim. These criminals want as much information on you as possible, and there is plenty of public information available today on almost everybody.

In separate instances, two social media influencers received similar calls—one from a man who demanded money, or else he would kill the sister, who was heard sobbing in the background. The other caller was a man threatening to kill the influencer's mother. These two influencers paid the thousand dollars being demanded by the callers.[14]

A grandfather received a call, allegedly from his grandson, who told the grandfather that he had been involved in a car accident and had broken his nose. The grandfather thought something sounded a bit off because the voice spoke slower than his grandson. He hung up and learned that his grandson was in school and had not been involved in an accident.[15]

If you receive one of these phone calls, the FBI suggests that you ask the caller a lot of questions about the alleged kidnapped victim, because there will be questions that the scammer will not be able to answer. Also be on the lookout for an unfamiliar area code or an international number. If you have another phone, call the alleged victim's phone or that of a friend or family member to try to verify that the person is okay.

The FBI issued a warning about malicious actors creating deepfake synthetic content by manipulating photographs or videos to target victims. They receive an increasing number of complaints about victims, including children, whose photos or videos were altered into explicit content and circulated on social media or pornographic websites for the purpose of harassing victims or extorting money.

Sometimes victims are unaware that this material is circulating, until it is brought to their attention by another person. If the malicious actors are extorting money, they will send the material directly to the victim and threaten to release it publicly unless the victim pays the amount of money demanded. The motives are always harassment, bullying, and extortion.

This activity may violate several federal criminal statutes, but the FBI warns the public that it is easy for malicious actors to use advanced technology for exploitation. There is simply too much content creation technology that is accessible to people involved in criminal activity. They warn to be cautious about things you post online or send through direct messaging and other online sites, because criminals are always looking for their next victim.

The FBI offers these precautionary recommendations:

- Monitor your children's online activity and discuss risks associated with sharing personal content. Anything posted can be captured, manipulated, and distributed without your knowledge or consent.

- Run frequent online searches of your and your children's information, including full name, address, and phone number, to identify any exposure.

- Set social media accounts to private, including your list of friends.

- Use reverse image search engines to locate any photos or videos that have circulated online without your knowledge.

- Exercise caution when accepting friend requests. Be wary of communicating, engaging in video conversations, or sending images to people you do not know and anybody you do not trust. Do not be pressured into sending photographs or images.

- Do not send money to unknown or unfamiliar individuals. Even if they have your photos or other content, giving them money will not guarantee they will not share it.

- Use caution when interacting with people online. Be careful about clicking on links in emails or private messages because this allows the scammer to hack your account. Hacked or fake accounts can be manipulated to gain trust, and then used to further criminal activity.
- Research the privacy, data sharing, and data retention policies of social media platforms, apps, and websites before uploading and sharing any personal content.[16]

Caller-ID spoofing is another crime that is on the rise. This is a process wherein a caller masks their own phone number and makes it appear on your caller ID that the call is coming from a number that is different from the caller's actual phone number. It is even possible to look at your caller ID and see a spoofed call coming in from your own phone number. The scammer will often use your own area code to make you think it's a local call. If you receive one of these calls, the FCC advises that you don't hang on; hang up!

The Federal Communications Commission says this about caller-ID spoofing:

> *"Spoofing is when a caller deliberately falsifies the information transmitted to your caller ID display to disguise their identity. Scammers often use neighbor spoofing so it appears that an incoming call is coming from a local number, or spoof a number from a company or a government agency that you may already know and trust. If you answer, they use scam scripts to try to steal your money or valuable personal information, which can be used in fraudulent activity."*[17]

In addition to learning how to protect yourself from malicious actors and taking appropriate precautions, you also should train yourself to discern the fakes when you see them. Christians, especially, are easily deceived because they want to believe that everybody tells the truth. Sometimes they're so deceived, they can be presented with the truth, and they will still believe the liar—even when the liar is someone they don't know. There was a day when almost everybody had integrity and honest motives. But today that is simply not the case, even with people who slap on the Christian label.

It is better to err on the side of caution than to believe everything we see and hear, especially if something seems unusual or out of order. We used to say, "Trust, but verify." These days we need to verify before we trust.

## CHAPTER 3

# THE SPIRIT BEHIND AI

Christ and His disciples were on their way to Jerusalem when they took a shortcut through the mountains of Samaria, where the Samaritans and the Jews had been engaged in a religious conflict for decades. When the citizens heard that Jesus, a Jew, and His Jewish disciples were passing through, they publicly challenged and rejected their ministry.

This caused negative emotions to surface among Christ's disciples. Two of the men, James and John, surnamed by Christ "the sons of thunder" (Mark 3:17), asked Christ if they should call fire down from heaven and consume them. Christ immediately rebuked them and said, "*You do not know what manner of spirit you are of*" (Luke 9:54-55 NKJV).

The same statement could be made concerning the motivating spirit behind artificial intelligence. In and of itself, technology is not evil; it depends on how the technology is used and the spirit behind it. A wrong spirit can take a good idea and generate a bad idea with intent to use it for unscrupulous purposes.

The same is true of money. Some people say money is the root of all evil, but that is not what the Bible says. It's the *love of money* that is the root of all evil, because longing for money has caused some to wander from the faith and experience many sorrows (1 Tim. 6:10). A hundred-dollar bill is amoral. People need money for food, clothing, fuel, and general living expenses. But people can take that same money and spend it on bad things, like illegal drugs or criminal enterprises that lead to bondage and death. These are evil uses of money, and people who lust after money will find ways to make people spend their money on evil things. The ways in which a person spends their money and the ways in which they influence other people to spend their money reflect the good or evil in their heart. They can have a wrong spirit.

When televisions first appeared in homes, there were silver antennas on the back that could be moved in different directions to pick up the station and clear static from the black and white picture on the screen. Some well-meaning Christians perceived that the metal box was a source of evil, at times calling the antennas "the devil's tail." But the television itself is just a box. It has no moral conscience regarding the images that appear on the screen, since the content originated in the minds of writers, with actors and producers creating the information the public views.

The internet is a perfect example of a technological invention that can be used for good or evil. Anybody with internet access and the knowledge to upload content can create a webpage or a video channel and produce whatever material they desire. If you start watching a particular topic on YouTube, the algorithms will continue to bring forth similar content. A person could binge watch for days on just one topic. If you search to find the number of channels on YouTube alone, you'll see numbers that range from 38 million to 373 million. Whatever the actual number might be, it's still astronomical. Millions of people create content. Some content is great, and some is terrible. Millions of people around the world watch on computers and electronic devices.

This reveals the impact of digital information. You can choose whether to create and watch content that generates spiritual and moral darkness, or content that turns up the light and diminishes darkness.

## POSITIVES AND NEGATIVES

Many people are rightly concerned about personal privacy issues as they relate to artificial intelligence, including concerns about how the systems are being used in the name of national security. Facial recognition, for example, has its positive and negative uses. In some ways, cameras in cities are seen as an invasion of privacy, while at the same time, facial recognition software can and has been used to deter crime and locate wanted criminals. People don't give it much thought when facial recognition is used for passport confirmation or when boarding and exiting cruise ships. But people understand that anything can be taken to the extreme and used against the public when nefarious actors are involved.

Tracking devices, such as those built into smartphones, have been used in the past to locate people who were missing. People have their dogs chipped in case they get lost. Members of royalty have chipped their children in case they are lost or kidnapped. While most people feel unsettled about such tracking technology, they are still glad when a missing person is found or when a crime is solved through tracking technology.

When questionable technology fulfills a positive purpose, we accept the technology. But in the back of our mind, we're wondering what else is planned for society using this technology, especially when it's placed in the wrong hands. Just ask the Chinese, who cannot travel or nod to a stranger without being tracked.

## READING YOUR MIND

Researchers at the University of Texas at Austin say they have successfully created an artificial intelligence system that can translate a person's brain activity into readable language. The device is called a semantic decoder, and it utilizes technology similar to that of ChatGPT. Thoughts transcribed onto paper from a person's mind have been imperfect, but still correct half the time.[18]

Most of us cannot image any scenario in which mind reading technology can be used for positive reasons. But somebody with a financial or social interest in the outcome will always try to convince us of a vital humanitarian need for the technology so that we will accept it, even begrudgingly.

Top security experts say there is a possible advantage to using mind reading AI technology for national security reasons. They say that somebody with the wrong thoughts could be forbidden from doing certain things, such as flying on a commercial airline. As people go through airport security, if AI reads their thoughts and does not approve, the person would not be permitted to board a plane.

Artificial intelligence could also read your body language, heart rate, eyes, and voice to determine if you are telling the truth when asked questions by security personnel. It could catch nervous fidgeting and other things that would arouse suspicion.

People who have nothing to hide might accept this technology because they are told that it will keep hijackers off the plane or ill-intentioned people out of public places. But what happens when someone decides that you should not be allowed on a plane or in a public venue because of your moral, political, or religious beliefs? If you think this cannot happen, you will learn in a later chapter how technology is already being used to deny freedom to certain people for those very reasons.

## KNOWLEDGE INCREASED

There is a small but powerful group of people in the world who believe that, if they can increase their knowledge and build technology based on that knowledge, one day they can create a new world and a utopian society. This will be a place with no barriers to tolerance and acceptance, so long as everybody thinks and acts in a government-approved manner. They desire a world where the planet is saved because nobody owns cows or cars, and fossil fuels stay underground where they belong. It will be a world where knowledge is limitless, and where they will live forever without aging, even if they must depopulate the earth and give up their own humanity to achieve these goals.

The spirit that motivates this group is the same spirit that tempts people with the desire to gain knowledge and abilities that surpass those of God Himself. Twenty-five hundred years ago in ancient Babylon, it was already predicted that the emphasis toward the time of the end would be increased knowledge: *"But you, Daniel, shut up the words, and seal the book until the time of the end; many shall run to and fro, and knowledge shall increase"* (Dan. 12:4).

In Genesis, there were many trees in the Garden of Eden. Some were for food, and others were for beauty and enjoyment. However, only two are mentioned by name. One was the *tree of life*, and the other was *the tree of the knowledge of good and evil* (Gen. 2:9). This word knowledge in Hebrew is *da'ath,* and it includes the idea of having cunning wit and understanding.

Eve's response to Satan's invitation of gaining concealed knowledge and wisdom is interesting. She saw that the tree was good for food, saw that it was pleasant to look at, believed the fruit would make her wiser, ate it herself, and offered it to Adam. Both had their eyes opened when they ate it.

The Almighty understood the danger of fallen humanity living forever with knowledge of evil. God stationed an angelic cherub to prevent access to the tree of life, "lest he put forth his hand and eat of the tree of life and live forever" (Gen. 3:22).

## THE KNOWLEDGE OF EVIL

In the right hands, knowledge of good can change the world in a positive manner. Consider all the ways our lives have improved over the last century through increased knowledge.

In the wrong hands, knowledge can destroy. The knowledge of evil can motivate a person or group of people who have destructive inclinations to tap into that knowledge and use it for nefarious purposes.

On August 6, 1945, the first nuclear bombs were dropped on the Japanese cities of Hiroshima and Nagasaki. Since that time, governments around the world have feared that rouge dictators will develop their own nuclear weapons. Occasionally a radical leader in the Middle East will publicly admit that he intends to use weapons of mass destruction against his country's enemies. Israel and the United States are always at the top of their enemy list.

During World War II, imagine if the Nazi military under Hitler's command had access to nuclear weapons. How might the outcome of the war have been different?

Saddam Hussein and his Baath Party were accused of gassing the Kurds and killing over five thousand people. With the weapons to do so, Saddam could have released chemical warfare against allied forces during the Gulf War conflict and killed tens of thousands of military personnel.

The message from the Garden of Eden is that Adam and Eve already had all the knowledge they needed. They had life, and the Almighty manifested His presence daily in the garden. They were oblivious to the knowledge of good versus evil and of how this forbidden knowledge would alter the course of human history. Everybody must now choose between the road leading to good or the road leading to evil. One is narrow and straight, and the other is a wide road that leads to destruction.

To ignore the dangers of the knowledge of evil leads toward conflict and trouble. There is something that I call a sin against knowledge. An example is the Babylonian King Nebuchadnezzar, who was warned in a spiritual dream that his pride would cost him the throne and his kingdom for seven years. He was given one year in which to change his ways and have things go well for him, or else continue to walk in arrogance and experience the fruit of evil. He chose unwisely. Twelve months after the warning, the king experienced a seven-year mental breakdown that ended with him living like an animal and eating grass like an ox. He had been warned, but he sinned against that knowledge.

The love of money, or we might say greed, is often the underlying spirit that motivates developers of new technology. Millions of dollars will be invested into different phases of this technology, and people will reap billions in return. Despite the warnings, some who stand to gain the most say the return is worth the risk.

The spirit behind much of AI, especially when it is used for control, manipulation, and knowledge beyond that which is humanly possible, is no different from the experience of the first couple. The lie presented was: Something is being withheld from you; there is more knowledge that will make you wiser and raise you to the level of God.

Scattered among today's AI experts are those who warn of potential dangers. Others don't care that the rapid expansion of knowledge, without the conscience to use it wisely, could lead down the path of evil, with no chance of return.

Despite Elon Musk's involvement in the advancement of AI, which includes the co-founding of OpenAI, he recently warned about the speed at which artificial intelligence is developing and the potential for destruction if placed in the wrong hands. He said, "There is a strong possibility that [artificial intelligence] will make life much better and that we'll have an age of abundance. And there's some chance that it goes wrong and destroys humanity."[19]

Geoffrey Hinton, a leading AI pioneer also said, "AI could pose an existential threat to humanity, and we should worry seriously about how we stop these things getting control over us."[20]

Microsoft chief economist Michael Schwarz said, "AI will likely be used by bad actors and could cause real damage."[21]

Members of The Center for AI Safety say that mitigating the risk of extinction from AI should be a global priority, because inventing machines that are more powerful than us is playing with fire. While AI has many beneficial applications, it can be used to perpetuate bias, power autonomous weapons, promote misinformation, and conduct cyberattacks. Even as AI systems are used with human involvement, AI agents are increasingly able to act autonomously to cause harm.[22]

In 2017, Vladimir Putin warned that, whoever becomes the leader in AI will become the ruler of the world. In these days of advanced knowledge and technology, which is unlike anything we have seen throughout history, the world should be concerned about who controls artificial intelligence. Indeed, that will determine who rules the world.

## CHAPTER 4

# TRANSHUMANISTS: THE GOD MAKERS

The human brain is a marvel. It weighs around three pounds and yet uses twenty percent of a person's oxygen and calories. It contains an estimated one hundred billion neurons. The brain is responsible for motor functions, cognitive functions, and involuntary functions. It controls both conscious and unconscious activities.

We have always heard that humans use ten percent or less of their brain capacity, but modern imaging now shows that was a myth. Brain function can be mapped with imaging techniques which indicate that all parts of the brain are active at different times. Some areas become more active, depending on the task being performed, but no area of the brain is inactive. A possible exception would be medical conditions resulting from issues such as traumatic brain injury.

In the antediluvian world, between the fall of Adam and the flood of Noah, the first ten generations from Adam to Noah lived hundreds of years. This gave each person the time needed to gain more knowledge and teach it to the next generation. Methuselah, the oldest human on record, stretched his lifespan to 969 years (Gen. 5:27). He died one week before the global cataclysmic deluge known as Noah's flood.

Living hundreds of years makes it possible for people to gain more knowledge, experience, and wisdom, thereby expanding the quantity and quality of information stored in the human mind. As millennia passed, and we witnessed the development of computers that store massive volumes of data, we now have a seemingly endless amount of knowledge and information available to us, much of it collected in one place. We are witnessing the time when we can enter a question into a computer application and, within seconds, receive an answer that might have taken days or months to acquire through traditional research.

## THE FINAL BATTLE

The Bible's prophetic scriptures introduced to the world a word that has been penned in newspapers and magazines, spoken during tragic news stories, and feared since the time it was first written. Around AD 95, that word was written on parchment when a prophetic visionary named John entered a spiritual trance and pierced the veil like a futuristic time traveler. He wrote about strange symbolism and life-threatening, destructive disasters that would come upon the earth one day.

Later generations of skeptics would call them the writings of a madman. However, John's predictions have been researched for centuries and considered true visions of things to come. The word that is known globally and tossed into the journalists' mix anytime the world seems in danger is *Armageddon.*

The word *Armageddon* is found in Revelation, the last book of the Bible. Revelation speaks of an apocalypse, a word which, in Greek, means "uncovering, unveiling, or revelation." Revelation 16:16 tells us the location for a final battle at a place called Armageddon and a hill called Mount Megiddo.

The mount or hill of Megiddo is a mound overlooking the Valley of Megiddo in Israel. The hill of Megiddo, which covers an area of about fifteen acres, is still under archaeological excavation. Over the course of five thousand years, a total of twenty cities were built over top of each other on the hill of Megiddo.

Historically, numerous battles were fought over control of those cities. Christians who believe that the book of Revelation is still to be fulfilled and who take the Bible literally believe that this will be the location of the world's final military campaign. It will involve two hundred million solders who will gather there days before the Messiah returns (Rev. 9:16; 16:16).

Prophetically, this final battle is centered in Israel's Valley of Megiddo, also called the Jezreel Valley. This conflict is not the only global battle, nor is it the most dangerous. Armageddon is focused in one nation, Israel. However, this new and controversial battle with artificial intelligence will impact every nation and person on earth.

The world is fascinated with the benefits presented to them by artificial intelligence; and indeed, there are many benefits. The technology advances at lightning speed, such that by the time this book has been printed, some things will already have changed. It is developing so quickly that it frightens some of its proponents and creators, as they warn of the need for immediate and appropriate global restrictions for the safety of humanity. We have been warned by some proponents of AI that people who refuse to go along with this technology will one day find themselves thrust back to a time when they will become useless and where they will be sharpening rocks to spear small animals for dinner.

Developers tell us that machines are so smart, they are outwitting and outperforming humans at an unprecedented rate. Since machines are allegedly becoming smarter and better equipped than humans, there is an obvious solution, they say. If you can't beat them, join them. Or, in this case, merge with them.

## MAN AND MACHINE

The philosophical and scientific movement that seeks to merge man with machine and to use sophisticated technologies that enhance longevity and cognition is called transhumanism. Some want to use technology to increase lifespan; for example, they suggest that gene-editing technology will cure diseases such as Parkinson's, Alzheimer's, and other currently incurable diseases. Others believe they can create an evolved human that will defy death and live forever.

Transhumanists seek ways for humanity to permanently move past our present physical, intellectual, and psychological limitations. This is defined as the ability to expand our minds to intellectual heights that are currently unreachable. It is defined as creating bodies that are resistant to disease and aging, bodies that never grow tired, and minds that never experience anxiety or other negative emotions. Transhumanists want to reach states of consciousness that the brain cannot currently access. Ultimately, they want the option to live forever, or at least as long as they choose, in this enhanced state.

A dichotomy exists between transhumanists who desire to live on a fallen earth forever and those in this same group who believe that the earth's population is too large and unsustainable. Why do they want humans to live forever if they believe there are already too many humans on the planet? Does this mean that only selective, wealthy individuals will be permitted to reach anticipated heights of intellectual genius and immortality?

That seems to be the opinion of Israeli historian, atheist, and author Yuval Noah Harari. He said the following in one of his many interviews available online:

> *"There will likely be economic inequality, because not everybody will be able to afford the cost to live forever. Economic inequality will be transformed into biological inequality. You've always had*

> *inequality, but it was social, economic, and political. It wasn't biological. Humankind will split into different biological casts. The rich will enjoy physical and mental abilities which will really be superior to the poor. And once such a gap opens, it becomes almost impossible to close it because the poor will no longer be able to compete with the rich."* [23]

Transhumanism is not a new idea. The word might first have been used by the biologist, Julian Huxley, who believed that the human species can transcend itself. Even Benjamin Franklin longed for a method of embalming so that a dead person might be recalled to life at any time in the future.

Elon Musk once said that people need to become cyborgs, defined as an organism with both biological and technological components. Cyborg abilities extend beyond normal human limitations. In science fiction, a cyborg is part human and part machine, but we are witnessing the day when this is no longer simply science fiction.

One way that technology giants believe they can merge man with machine is by using implants that fall under the umbrella of brain-computer interfaces (BCI). Initially, at least, their plan is to use the implants to benefit people with certain medical conditions.

Here is how Musk's company, Neuralink, and its product called neural lace was introduced several years ago at the Global Manufacturing and Industrialization Summit:

> *"In 2017 [Musk] launched Neuralink, a medical research company that aims to unite the human brain with intelligent computers using the concept of 'neural lace'. Neural lace is a form of Brain-Computer Interface (BCI) which facilitates a direct communication pathway between an enhanced or 'wired brain' and an external device. In practice, neural lace is an ultra-thin mesh with a collection of electrodes capable of monitoring brain function and facilitating direct computing capabilities*

> *from thought. It is inserted through the skull using a tiny needle containing the rolled-up mesh which unravels spanning the brain. Once in place, the interface uses signals from the brain to enable communication and control applications through thinking alone. As part of the rapidly advancing field of artificial intelligence (AI), neural lace technology could allow people to become an "AI-Human symbiote" enhancing cognition as our brains become part of AI and change the way we go about our lives."* [24]

At the World Government Summit in Dubai, Elon Musk suggested that there is a path to having some sort of merger of biological intelligence and machine intelligence. Musk suggests that the features of neural link technology will transform the medical world to benefit people with neurological diseases such as Parkinson's.

New developments that provide medical assistance for people with terrible diseases or for those who need artificial limbs can serve as a positive example for the use of technology, if you don't mind having an object injected into your skull and unraveled over your brain. However, this is one of those technologies that can easily be used for evil when placed in the wrong hands. Some of the technologies being developed or discussed today give us clear indications that, in the wrong hands, this same technology could help fulfill the prophecies of the beast system that John saw in Revelation.

From the Global Manufacturing and Industrialization Summit, we are offered this disconcerting summary of neural lace: "Neural Lace is a next generation brain-computer interface (BCIs) that could *change the way people think and communicate*, and even be the answer to debilitating neurological disorders." How many people want something unraveled in their brain that changes the way they think and communicate, based on someone else's definition of proper thoughts and communication?

## THE QUEST FOR ETERNAL LIFE

Modern humanity is in a technological quest for eternal life, and they are certain they've found the answer in artificial intelligence. Some, such as Yuval Noah Harari, believe that death itself can be killed. He says this about the goal of defeating death:

> *"People avoided the issue of death because the goal seemed too elusive. Why create unreasonable expectations? We're now at a point, however, where we can be frank about it. The leading project of the Scientific Revolution is to give humankind eternal life. Even if killing death seems a distant goal, we have already achieved things that were inconceivable a few centuries ago...*
>
> *"A few serious scholars suggest that by 2050, some humans will become a-mortal (not immortal, because they could still die of some accident, but a-mortal, meaning that in the absence of fatal trauma their lives could be extended indefinitely)."* [25]

Others who speak of eternal life think of it as "an artificial intelligence so advanced that it immortalizes people by 'remembering' their entire experience."[26] Harari also imagines that humans will be able to back up their brains to a hard drive and then run the brains on a laptop. He wonders if your laptop would then be able to think and feel like a Sapien, and could a digital mind be created that would have a sense of self, consciousness, and memory?

One goal focuses on creating physical eternal life; the other focuses on creating computers that will remember someone so accurately as to make the person immortal.

We already leave a large digital footprint. For instance, anything we post on the internet will never die. Photographs tell your life story, and some people can't resist posting pictures of absolutely everything, from the food they ate for dinner to the selfie in front of the public restroom mirror. Financial transactions leave a footprint. Deeds of ownership leave a footprint. Your credit card tells where you've been and what you've purchased. People would be surprised to learn how much information about themselves is available online.

The digital immortality that transhumanists speak of goes even further. This begins when a person intentionally sits in front of a camera or digital device and records everything about their life. This might be beneficial for researchers of well-known or influential people long after those individuals are deceased. It might be interesting for a family member to look back on the lives of their parents or grandparents after they are gone. But few people are going to care about the plethora of information compiled in a person's digital immortality file after the person has died.

Gordon Bell, a retired veteran of the information technology industry and a former researcher at Microsoft, set out years ago to capture and record every memory of his life. His goal was not to put his life on the internet for everybody to read, but to memorialize it for personal reasons. Bell stored everything possible on a large database: videos of lectures he had given, CDs, correspondence, photos, images of websites he visited, and television shows he watched. He even started wearing a camera around his neck that took a picture every thirty seconds.[27]

Bell, who is now eighty-eight years old, stopped recording when he realized two things. First, the project was not bringing a lot of value to his life. Second, it was hard to manage the terabytes of data this volume of information generated. Bell decided it was hard to bring all that information together. And besides, nobody wanted it.

In 2016, Bell said that he believes artificial intelligence will eventually be able to organize all our captured data and free us from data overload. He envisions an application that will allow us to ask a question about our past and receive an answer from a virtual assistant.[28]

That was Bell's vision seven years ago. It wouldn't take much for artificial intelligence to fulfill that vision. Tech developers are already working on quantum computers that will, among many other things, help people live forever digitally. Within the last four years, a couple of new developments indicate that this day is just around the corner.

First, Google revealed that they now have a Sycamore quantum computer that could solve a math problem in two hundred seconds that would take ten thousand years on the world's fastest supercomputer. China claimed that they have a quantum computer that is 100 trillion times faster than an ordinary supercomputer.[29]

This idea of a supercomputer to beat all supercomputers thrills scientists, technology developers, and transhumanists. They are convinced that this will enable them to find a cure for every disease and a solution to every world problem. If only computers could operate at a speed unattainable by the human mind, imagine what they could accomplish.

At this point, it appears that technology's definition of eternal life is closer to Yuval Harari's vision—living forever, or at least as long as you choose, in a utopian society designed by a small group of elitists who have one goal. That goal is to control the world and its assets, and to enslave most of the people in it.

## LIFESPAN ACCORDING TO SCRIPTURE

The biological rules for the length of human life are found throughout the Bible. For sixteen hundred years before the flood of Noah, people from Seth's linage lived long lives, some over nine hundred years. Later the life span was reduced. In Psalm chapter 90, Moses wrote that our days shall be seventy and by reason of strength eighty, and that we should number our days and gain wisdom during our time on the earth. This doesn't mean that nobody will live beyond the age of eighty, although it is rare to find people who live to age ninety or a hundred.

A shorter lifespan is believed to be a result of people spreading evil instead of good, and thereby influencing others to sin. The primary example is God allowing the flood because He had to separate two groups of people. The world was being morally and spiritually corrupted by evildoers so that only Noah was found to be righteous.

The tree of life in the Garden of Eden was planted by God Himself. According to Scripture, the tree of life originated in God's celestial Heaven and is found in the heavenly paradise. In John's vision, he noted that this tree bears twelve different types of fruit and yields its fruit each month. The leaves of the tree are for the healing of the nations (Rev. 2:7; 22:2). This unusual fruit sustained the inhabitants of Eden by renewing their bodies and creating a continuous and supernatural cycle of renewal. It was called the tree of life because eating it produced an endless life.

The story of Adam and Eve forfeiting eternal life on Earth must have been handed down for generations, because all ancient people in Mesopotamia knew that it once had been possible to live forever. Ancient kings, rulers, and even some Roman emperors were often deified and considered gods, some believing they could be reincarnated into another life after they died. Of course, none of them managed to accomplish that feat. All eventually died and were buried and memorialized in their tombs, where their remains were discovered thousands of years later.

## THE AFTERLIFE

The afterlife was a prominent theme among the Egyptians. Rulers and the very wealthy were mummified, as this was believed to assist in their journey after death. Objects were placed in their tombs because it was believed these would be used in the next life. Also placed in the tomb was a small image in the likeness of a pharaoh. The legend was that this lesser god would assist the dead in their journey through the underworld to the next life.

Items that have been found in tomb excavations include furniture, wooden objects covered in gold, pottery, and even gold objects of great value. Also found are ordinary items such as storage jars, flint knives, and ivory combs. Various amulets were placed on the body and held in place by mummy wrappings, in the belief that these would protect the deceased.

When tombs were discovered and excavated, two things become evident. First, none of the belongings were transported to another world. Second, the mummified remains were still in the coffin and had not been raised in an afterlife.

Neither their lesser gods nor their greater gods had the power to raise the dead. After six thousand years of recorded history, humans are no closer to shutting down the exit on the road to death than Satan is to becoming like God. Yet, that doesn't stop mortal men from continuing to seek a fountain of youth that will keep them from aging and breathing their last breath.

## AI AND ETERNAL LIFE

An inescapable law was established and reaffirmed thousands of years ago. After eating from the forbidden tree, God told Adam and Eve, *"From dust you were taken, and to dust you shall return"* (Gen. 3:19). Paul reaffirmed this when he wrote, *"It is appointed unto men once to die, and after this the judgment"* (Heb. 9:27). Death is unavoidable.

We hear fanciful discussions advancing the theory that certain types of AI could hold the missing key to man's search for the fountain of youth and immortality. Cryonics is one strange example of the search for immortality.

Cryonics is the process wherein people, immediately after death, have their bodies or heads frozen to extremely cold temperatures and placed in large metal tanks, in hopes that future technology will bring them back to life. True stories that read like your worst nightmare have been written about the condition of these bodies when they accidentally thaw out, or when the freezing process doesn't work properly. Some transhumanists think that frozen heads can someday have the brain revived and attached to a new body or a robot. They also believe that any diseased organs will be replaced with new artificial organs.[30] Cryonics is not too popular, but some assume they have nothing to lose by trying.

People who are spending their money on cryonics should look for a better investment. Nobody will be brought back to life by science after being frozen for decades. Before your body is ever frozen, you will have reached your destination. At that point, you aren't going anywhere until you stand before God on Judgment Day.

## AI WILL FAIL TO BRING IMMORTALITY

Most followers of Christ don't have a desire to live hundreds of years, or even a hundred years, on a fallen earth. They don't want to be frozen and brought back to life two hundred years from now. We already have the promise of eternal life in a place of utopia, and after a certain age, most believers are looking forward to that future life. It seems to be only the atheists who want to live on this earth forever, and they desire to create a perfect environment that only God Himself can provide. Perhaps they want to live forever because, despite not believing in a hereafter, they still fear what the hereafter holds.

Promotors of the AI eternal life theory miss another key that makes immortality in this human body impossible. Every living person, regardless of age, is a three-part creation. Each has a spirit, soul, and physical body (1 Thess. 5:23). Technology cannot recreate that. The life of the flesh is in the blood, and without blood in the body, life ceases (Lev. 17:11).

Most technology innovators don't believe in the validity of the Bible because they are atheists or agnostics, but the biblical revelation on death is simple. Death occurs once the human soul and spirit leave the physical body. The body without the spirit is dead (James 2:26). Paul confirmed this when he wrote, *"To be absent from the body is to be present with the Lord"* (2 Cor. 5:8).

Death is controlled by a divine appointment, a set date in which the spirit within the person is separated from the body. After this separation, the only thing left is a shell of flesh and bone. If revival or resurrection of a dead person's frozen body through AI methods were even possible, it would only make the body a science-fiction style robot. It would not be the person who died, the person whose personality and character left with the spirit that departed. It is impossible to replicate a human spirit, as this comes directly from God Himself at the moment of conception.

The soul also leaves the body at death. The Hebrew word for soul is *nephesh*, and it is the inner force that gives the person life and emotions. At creation, when God formed Adam from the dust, He breathed into Adam's nostrils the breath of life, and man became a living soul (Gen. 2:7). The word *soul* is written over four hundred times in the Old Testament, and all but two times the word *nephesh* is used. Both animals and humans have the breath of life that ceases at death.

Unshakable spiritual laws cannot be altered or broken. Law number one is that *"it is appointed unto men once to die, and after this the judgment"* (Heb. 9:27). The word *appointed* means that it has been laid up in reserve. Physical death is inevitable.

The second unbreakable law is the promise of an appointed number of years—generally, seventy to eighty. There is a time to live and a time to die (Eccl. 3:1-2). Your personal days are already set and numbered, and God alone controls them. Psalm 90:12 states, "*Teach us to number our days, that we might apply ourselves to wisdom.*" David, who could have been slain many times by wild animals or by Saul in battle wrote, "*God, take me not away in the midst of my days*" (Psa. 102:24).

The body of flesh ages and becomes weaker. One day life ends, causing the flesh and bones to return to the dust of the earth (Gen. 2:7). The only way a dead body can come to life again is if the spirit and soul return to the same physical body from which it left. This happens when God divinely and supernaturally raises someone from the dead, or when a person who has not been dead long is brought back to life through immediate medical intervention, such as cardiopulmonary resuscitation.

Once the blood is gone, and certainly once the person is embalmed or frozen, science and technology will not bring that person back to life. No matter how hard they try, innovators of AI will never be able to create a new soul and spirit nor bring the soul and spirit of the deceased back to an artificially created body.

Eternal life will *never* be created, controlled, or managed through artificial intelligence. However, during the Great Tribulation, there will be a walking, talking, moving, living image that will be created by man and worshipped for a short time. Before doubting that a global generation could worship a manmade image, remember that entire religions, some with billions of followers, already build temples to carved images, leaving a gift as an offering, and praying before a graven image of a false god.

## CHAPTER 5

# DNA MANIPULATION: CREATING DEMIGODS

When people talk about transhumanism and the convergence of the human mind and computers, I cannot help but think of genetic modification. The idea of genetically modified humans dates to over five thousand years ago as an experiment in ancient history. A race of demigods was created throughout the Middle East who were considered part human and part divine. It was a form of genetic manipulation to disrupt a plan of the Almighty God, to bring to Earth a perfect, sinless man who would have the power to redeem humanity back to God and into a position of being a child of God.

This ancient genetic modification resulted in the procreation of an entire race of giants, some of whom were called Nephilim and Rephaim in the Hebrew Scriptures. This is one of the great mysteries in the Bible, and it is often untaught or misunderstood. However, there are biblical and historical writings that indicate these giants existed. After their destruction, they became the theme of legends in Greek mythology. In Genesis 3:15, these giant men were first called *the seed of the serpent.*

That ancient battle was a clash between two kingdoms and two ideologies, one clothed in light and the other motivated by darkness. The story reads like a Hollywood movie script. However, the outcome of this peculiar genetic modification was set for destruction.

## GIANTS AND ALIENS

Some of the highest rated documentaries on television feature interviews with alleged experts explaining their numerous theories on the existence of ancient aliens. Edited into the program are painted images of figures drawn or carved on walls of ancient tombs or caverns, along with strange objects found among excavated ruins. Experts claim that these other-worldly beings are aliens who visited Earth from planets that are light-years away. Some go so far as to say that these were cosmic gods that once visited Earth on reverse-engineered space craft. But what does the Bible say?

One of the greatest ancient mysteries in the Bible is that of the fallen angels and a race of giant men that once lived on Earth. There was a time when angels were sent to Earth in human form, which became the time when some suggest that "gods became men."

The first biblical report of angels and giant men was recorded by Moses around thirty-five hundred years ago:

> *"Now it came to pass, when men began to multiply on the face of the earth, and daughters were born to them, that the sons of God saw the daughters of men, that they were beautiful; and they took wives for themselves of all whom they chose."*
>
> – Genesis 6:1-2 NKJV

> *"There were giants on the earth in those days, and also afterward, when the sons of God came in to the daughters of men and they bore children to them. Those were the mighty men who were of old, men of renown."*
>
> – Genesis 6:4 NKJV

These two verses reveal that the giant men were created through reproduction, and it began in ancient times, before the flood of Noah. The phrase *sons of God*, or in Hebrew, *Bnei Elohim*, is used five times in

Genesis 6:2, 6:4, and Job 1:6, 2:1, and 38:7. In the book of Job, the sons of God are identified as angels who are standing at God's throne, preparing to minister on the earth. In Job 38:7, the term *sons of God* refers to angels that were present and rejoicing together when God created Earth.

The story of angels and their relationship with the beautiful daughters of men is one of the Bible's most unusual and intriguing narratives.

## PRE-FLOOD ANGELS TEACHING MEN

Why did God send angels to Earth to appear as men during this time? Jewish history and early church fathers provide details about this event.

After the fall of Adam, the earth's population grew until there was a shortage of teachers to instruct the people and explain how to follow God. Jewish belief is that, in the twenty-five hundred years from Adam to Moses, there were no written commandments from God and no written revelation from Him for mankind to follow. Yet, God desired to teach men righteousness and holy living.

To do so, He commissioned a select group of angels to descend to Earth and take on human form, in order that they could be seen and heard by the people on Earth. These angels were to teach the people, face-to-face, the secrets of Heaven and Earth, along with the rules of God.

While these angels were in a human body, they could fully function as any other human. Over time, the angels became enamored by the beautiful daughters of men. They eventually broke the rules of nature by taking the women as wives and producing an offspring of men who were enormous in size and strength, known in Scripture as giants. The Hebrew word for giants in Genesis 6:4 is *Nephilim*. These Nephilim rapidly began to appear on the earth, until they created great fear in the hearts of the people.

The unnatural creation of giants from the seed of angels explains the Scripture where God said that there would be a "seed of the serpent," or a satanic seed that would be upon the earth. Speaking about the serpent, God said, *"And I will put enmity* [hatred and hostility] *between you and the woman, and between your seed and her Seed* [Messiah]" (Gen. 3:15).

The book of Jubilees (sometimes called the Lesser Genesis) was known in the first century and is mentioned by early Jewish sources. It was used and quoted by the Essenes, the community of men living in Qumran prior to the destruction of the temple in AD 70. In the book of Jubilees, we find an account of the binding of the angels that were sent to Earth and sinned:

> *"And it came to pass when the sons of men began to increase on the earth, and daughters were born to them that in the first year of the jubilee that the angels of God looked on them and saw that they were beautiful; and they took wives from them as many as they chose. And they bore them sons: and they became giants... And against the angels He had sent on earth His anger was so great that he uprooted them from their dominion and commanded us to imprison them in the depths of the earth; and behold they are in prison there and separate."*
>
> – Jubilees 5:1-6

The book of Jubilees confirms the Genesis Scriptures, and also the account of the Apostle Peter, who wrote that these angels were *"cast down to hell and delivered into chains of darkness, to be reserved unto judgment"* (2 Peter 2:4).

This genetic manipulation caused by the mingling of the seed was creating the possibility that all flesh would become corrupt, thus endangering the bloodline of the promised future Messiah (Gen. 3:15). Moses wrote, *"God saw the wickedness of man was great in the earth and that every imagination and the thoughts of his heart were evil continually*" (Gen. 6:5). The Hebrew word for imagination is *yester*, and it refers to something formed or created, but figuratively can allude to conception. The idea here is that a person conceives (births) thoughts in their heart, and in Noah's day they conceived evil. And they did so collectively, twenty-four hours a day without stopping.

Many of these evil imaginations were being fueled by the giant men who were being conceived from the seed of the angels who were sent to Earth as humans. All of their offspring had corrupt DNA, which we might describe today as genetic modification. This reproductive manipulation was not only affecting the bloodline of humans, but a careful look at specific phrases in Genesis hints that some form of manipulation involved animals. It reads, "*all flesh had corrupted itself*" (Gen. 6:12). God warned, "*I will destroy man and beast... for I am sorry that I have made them*" (Gen. 6:7).

Based on this reading, it is likely that the perversion of these genetically corrupt giants had spread to include bestiality, an abominable sin under the Law of God, that if committed led to a death penalty (Lev. 20:15). *All flesh* included both man and beast. The corrupt condition brought complete moral and spiritual depravity, to the point that no option remained for God except to purge the earth and destroy humans, beasts, and of course, the demigods called giants.

The book of Jasher is mentioned twice in the Bible (Josh. 10:13; 2 Sam. 1:18), and it elaborates on the idea of intentional genetic corruption in the animal kingdom. Notice it mentions that this mixture of species was done to provoke the Lord. A section on the days of Noah reads:

> "*And the sons of men in those days took from the cattle of the earth, the beasts of the field and the fowls of the air, and taught the mixture of animals of one species with the other, in order*

*wherewith to provoke the Lord; and God saw that the whole earth was corrupt, for all flesh had corrupted its ways upon earth, all men and all animals."*

– JASHER 4:18

## MIXING THE SEED OF HUMANS AND ANIMALS

Some secular researchers believe that "aliens" became involved with procreation by combining the alien seed with animals, thus producing strange-looking creatures with a human body and an animal's head or an animal's body with a human head. Ancient images have been found carved on stone in places like Persia, Iraq, and Egypt that show these kinds of odd figures.

From Scripture and historical writings, we know that these were not "aliens." We can say with near certainty that this strange breed of creatures that were both animal and human were birthed when the race of giants mixed their corrupted seed with that of the perfect animals that God had created.

Some suggest that characters of Greek mythology are based upon this genetic mixture of part human and part animal. That will be discussed later in this chapter.

## MODERN PARALLELS

The function of DNA and genetics was unknown among men in the days of Lot. However, when reading this narrative, we see a prophetic parallel in our time with the genetic manipulation of animal and human DNA.

One example is mice, which are humanized in a research laboratory so they can be used in medical research and in the testing of disease therapies. What is a humanized mouse? The Jackson Laboratory gives us this definition:

> *"Humanized mouse is a general term that refers to a mouse that has been engrafted with something from a human. This could be a short strand of human DNA, human tissue, a human tumor, a humanized immune system, or parts of the human microbiome."* [31]

Modern researchers have also experimented on animals with the intent to clone an exact genetic copy of an animal. The most famous cloned animal was a sheep named Dolly. The website for the National Human Genome Research Institute says this about animal cloning:

> *"Over the last 50 years, scientists have conducted cloning experiments in a wide range of animals using a variety of techniques. In 1979, researchers produced the first genetically identical mice by splitting mouse embryos in the test tube and then implanting the resulting embryos into the wombs of adult female mice. Shortly after that, researchers produced the first genetically identical cows, sheep and chickens by transferring the nucleus of a cell taken from an early embryo into an egg that had been emptied of its nucleus.*
>
> *"It was not until 1996, however, that researchers succeeded in cloning the first mammal from a mature (somatic) cell taken from an adult animal. After 276 attempts, Scottish researchers finally produced Dolly, the lamb from the udder cell of a 6-year-old sheep. Two years later, researchers in Japan cloned eight calves from a single cow, but only four survived.*
>
> *"Besides cattle and sheep, other mammals that have been cloned from somatic cells include: cat, deer, dog, horse, mule, ox, rabbit*

*and rat. In addition, a rhesus monkey has been cloned by embryo splitting."* [32]

That same website says there is "currently no solid scientific evidence that anyone has cloned human embryos." The idea of cloning humans is so ethically and morally repugnant that, if this research is currently being conducted somewhere in the world, those involved would never publicize it. They would do everything in their power to keep their work hidden.

There are three different types of cloning:

- Gene cloning, which creates copies of genes or segments of DNA;
- Reproductive cloning, which creates copies of whole animals;
- Therapeutic cloning, which creates embryonic stem cells. Researchers say they hope to use these cells to grow healthy tissue to replace injured or diseased tissues in the human body.[33]

Another form of genetic research involves genetic engineering or modification. We know, for example, that most of our food has been genetically modified. The National Human Genome Research Institute defines genetic engineering as:

*"...a process that uses laboratory-based technologies to alter the DNA makeup of an organism. This may involve changing a single base pair, deleting a region of DNA, or adding a new segment of DNA. For example, genetic engineering may involve adding a gene from one species to an organism from a different species to produce a desired trait."* [34]

Read that again: "Altering the DNA makeup of an organism" and "adding a gene from one species to an organism from a different species." Does that remind you of another time in history when giants roamed the earth?

The following information about human genome editing is found on the World Health Organization website:

> *"Genome editing is a method for making specific changes to the DNA of a cell or organism. It can be used to add, remove or alter DNA in the genome. Human genome editing technologies can be used on somatic cells (non-heritable), germline cells (not for reproduction) and germline cells (for reproduction).*
>
> *"Heritable human genome editing refers to editing of nuclear DNA in a way that may be heritable across generations. Heritable human genome editing is the subject of intense debate over its possible consequences for offspring and for society in general. They may pose greater safety and ethical issues than somatic human genome editing."* [35]

What might be the "possible consequences for offspring and for society in general?" What are the safety and ethical issues? Is this eerily reminiscent of the genetic experimentation and corruption that happened during the days of Noah? What are people hoping to create in the 21st century with genetic editing and DNA modification? Is it all being done to cure disease, as they claim?

The desire to alter DNA and genes of plants, animals, and humans knows no end, and the research in this field has exploded. Perhaps you've heard of a living organism gene-editing technology called CRISPR, an acronym for "Clustered Regularly Interspaced Short Palindromic Repeats." CRISPR technology cuts, customizes, and pastes pieces of genetic material, such as DNA.

Advance Biosciences proclaims that gene editing "creates exciting new possibilities within the life sciences for the therapeutic treatments of genetic disorders and cancer immunotherapy." Regeneron, another company that "perfects novel technologies like CRISPR and gene-silencing" states that "we don't shy away from a scientific challenge because we know nothing is out of bounds."

This is another area that is expected to advance rapidly with the production and use of quantum computers. There are said to be over ten thousand diseases believed to be caused by mutations of a single human gene, and scientists believe that faster computers, used in conjunction with technology such as CRISPR, could cure many or all such diseases.

An article published on October 31, 2020 in the New York Times warned that CRISPR gene editing can cause unwanted changes in human embryos by prompting them to discard large chunks of their genetic material. Nicole Kaplan, a geneticist at New York University, advised that "with the amount of power we hold, it is crucial to understand consequences we didn't intend."[36]

The same article mentioned that in 2018, a Chinese scientist named He Jiankui used Crispr-Cas9 technology to yield the world's first gene-edited infants. He altered the CCR5 gene in human embryos with the goal of conferring immunity to HIV. The doctor was found guilty of conducting illegal medical practices and sentenced to three years in prison. The experiment was widely condemned because the many ways in which gene editing technology can affect cells remain poorly understood.[37]

Jiankui is out of prison now and has opened a new biotechnology company in Beijing to focus on gene therapies. The therapies are said not to include the editing of human embryos.

Massachusetts Institute of Technology reported on June 28, 2023 that researchers have uncovered a new CRISPR-like system in animals that can edit the human genome. They reported that Fanzor, "the first RNA-guided DNA-cutting enzyme found in eukaryotes, could one day be harnessed to edit DNA more precisely than CRISPR/Cas systems." Fanzor is a protein that uses RNA as a guide to target DNA, and the

"Fanzors can be reprogrammed to edit the genome of human cells."[38]

The theory has also been discussed that parents will eventually be able to use gene editing technology to choose traits and features of a child, such as eye or hair color and other traits of physical appearance. These are dubbed "designer babies." While some argue that it would be nearly impossible to engineer a designer baby with specific characteristics, we can be sure that, if there's a way, scientists will find it and probably are already working on it.

Experimentation knows no end. Once scientists and researchers develop a new technology, they don't know when to stop. As Regeneron says, "Nothing is out of bounds."

Once we learn about the history of giants in biblical times, we can read the news headlines today and clearly understand Christ's end time warning: "*For as were the days of Noah, so will be the coming of the Son of Man*" (Matt. 24:37).

## NOAH AND HIS UNTAINTED DNA

Two lineages from Adam are mentioned in the Bible—the evil side of the lineage of their son Cain, who killed his brother Abel, and that of Cain's brother Seth, whose descendants were righteous.

Seth's lineage produced Enosh, and in his day, men began to call upon the name of the Lord (Gen. 4:26). Another descendent of Seth was Enoch, the seventh man from Adam, who fathered Methuselah at age sixty-five, then walked with God three hundred years before God took him (Gen. 5:21-22). The tenth generation from Adam gave us Noah, a righteous man who was "perfect in his generations" (Gen. 6:9).

Before God sent the flood, the procreation of giants had caused all flesh to become corrupt (Genesis 6:12). Because of the relentless evil, wickedness, and flesh corruption, God had no choice but to wipe all creation off the face of the earth, except Noah and his wife, their three sons, and their three wives.

Noah, who was perfect in his generations, found grace in the eyes of the Lord (Gen. 6:8-9). The Hebrew word for grace is *chen,* which is spelled with two Hebrew letters—chet and nun. The Hebrew name Noah is spelled *Noach* in Hebrew, and his name is chen spelled backwards with the letters nun and chet. Noah's name means *rest.* We read that Noah was a "just man" (Gen. 6:9). The word "*just*" in Hebrew is *tsaddiq*, meaning "a righteous person"—one who is in right standing with God, which also implies innocence. Noah was "perfect in his generations" (Gen. 6:9). The word *perfect* identifies him as being upright and without spot or blemish, morally and spiritually. It also means "undefiled."

In this context, God was also emphasizing that Noah was *undefiled by the corruption*, meaning that neither he nor his family had experienced DNA or genetic corruption, because they had not participated in the procreation of giant offspring. Everyone else on earth, in some form, had been corrupted and defiled by the wickedness of fallen angels and giants.

The Cain lineage became part of the seed of Satan, while Noah's lineage was from the seed of Seth. Being perfect meant that his blood line, from Adam to himself, had not been contaminated by the DNA or the seed of the giants. Imagine God looking throughout the entire earth and finding only one man who could be selected as a man of God to save his family from destruction.

## GIANTS AND IDOL WORSHIP

One of the perplexing biblical and historical questions is, "When or how did idolatry originate?" There is no biblical record of idols prior to Noah's flood. God gave the first warning against worshipping false gods to Israel after they departed Egypt. The Egyptians were worshippers of numerous gods, as were the Assyrians, Babylonians, and even the Greeks and Romans.

While this explanation of the origin of idolatry may seem too simplistic, there is a belief that the giants and their offspring, both before and after the flood, became legends (called "men of renown" in Genesis 6:4). Several early church fathers indicate that both the giants and their children were given names, and that centuries later, they were worshipped as gods. Justin Martyr, who lived from the years AD 100 to 165 wrote:

> *"(God) committed the care of men and all things under heaven to angels whom he appointed over them. But the angels transgressed this appointment, and were captivated by the love of women, and begot children who were those that are called demons; and besides, they afterwards subdued the human race to themselves, partly by teaching them to offer sacrifices, and incense and libations, of which they stood in need after they were enslaved by lustful passions; and among them they sowed murders, wars, adulteries, intemperate deeds, and all wickedness.*
>
> *"Whence also the poets and mythologists not knowing that it was the angels and those demons whom had been begotten by them did these things to men, and women, and cities, and nations which they related, ascribed them to god himself, and to those who were accounted to be his very offspring, and to the offspring of those who were called brothers, Neptune and Pluto, and to the children again of these their offspring. For whatever name each of the angels had given himself and his children, by that name they were called them."* [39]

Early cities were often named after their founders. Cain built a city and named it after his son. Sacred Jewish history indicates that even the cities in Canaan, such as Sodom, Gomorrah, Admah, and Zeboiim were names of the sons of Canaan, the youngest son of Ham, who was one of Noah's sons (Gen. 4:17; 14:2; 10:6).

Likewise, when people became enamored with these fallen angels and their giant offspring, they named their man-made idols after the names of the giants and their children. The Greeks, Romans, and Egyptians were polytheistic, meaning they believed in and worshipped many gods.

Mythologists constructed an elaborate genealogical lineage as they attempted to trace the heavenly visitors and place them as gods over events, planets, and the cosmos. Some of the Greek mythological gods and the connections Greeks believed they had to the earth, sky, or cosmic heavens were:

- Apollo — god of crops, herds, and divine distance; son of Zeus
- Artemis — goddess of the hunt, wild animals, and childbirth; daughter of Zeus
- Hera — sister-wife of Zeus; queen of the Olympian gods
- Zeus — god of the sky, weather, lightning and thunder
- Ares — god of war; an Olympic diety; son of Zeus and Hera
- Poseidon| — brother of Zeus; god of the sea and water; name means "lord of the earth"

The Romans rebranded the Greek gods and changed their names. Romans assigned a god to each planet that was visible in the sky. Planets in our solar system were given names of Roman gods; for example,

Jupiter, Mars, Venus, and Mercury were also names the Romans gave to their gods. It is possible that these fallen angels took to themselves the original names of these planets, and then the people, in turn and unknowingly, named the planets after them.

The New Testament indicates there were angels who did not keep their first estate, meaning their original domain and purpose: "And the angels who did not keep their proper domain, but left their own abode, He has reserved in everlasting chains under darkness for the judgment of the great day" (Jude 6 NKJV). Peter also told us that "God did not spare the angels who sinned, but cast them down to hell and delivered them into chains of darkness, to be reserved for judgment" (2 Peter 2:4 NKJV).

According to one tradition, one of the leading angels after the flood was named Azazel. The book of Enoch (the Ethiopian translation) records that these fallen angels were bound and placed in hell, under God's instruction to Michael the archangel and one of the seven chief angels named Raphael:

> *"Further God said to Raphael, 'Bind Azazel by his hands and his feet...And split open the desert which is in Deudael, and throw him in there. And cover him with darkness; and let him stay there forever...that on the Day of Judgment he may be hurled into the fire.' And God said unto Michael, 'Go inform Shemyaza and the other with him...when all their sons kill each other, and when they see the destruction of their beloved ones, bind them for seventy generations under the hill of the earth until the Day of Judgment...and in those days they will lead them to the abyss of fire."*
>
> – Book of Enoch (Ethiopian translation), Section 1 Chapter 10

Again, to be clear, the angels referred to in these verses are those who were sent to teach men righteousness. But they sinned and birthed of a race of giants that caused so much widespread corruption, God had to wipe people off the earth and start over.

These angels, originally assigned to Earth in human form before they birthed giants and were confined in hell, were then considered "gods" that had come from another galaxy to the pre-flood and again to the post-flood generations. It is my opinion that these are the creatures which are being called aliens by people in positions of power.

The giant men from Noah's day perished during the flood. Genesis 6:4 recognized one group before the flood and another group after the flood. How did they reappear after the flood?

The Bible doesn't answer that question, but according to Jewish tradition, a second group of angels were sent to Earth, appearing on Mount Hermon (northern Israel) with the same assignment as the previous group. This group also failed in their mission, falling into the second category of "fallen angels" who reproduced another race of giants.

Following the flood, as Earth's population grew, there were numerous groups of giants surrounding the Promised Land (see 1st and 2nd Samuel). An entire valley was named the Valley of Rephaim, which is a name given to one group of giants that returned after the flood (2 Sam. 5:18, 22; 23:13 and other references).

Three thousand years ago, when David took out the giant named Goliath, his mighty men slew four other giants living in southern Israel. The mention of giants disappeared from later biblical records, although there has been plenty of evidence that giants existed in other places throughout the world, including the United States.

In Genesis 11, by the time construction was stopped on the Tower of Babel and men were scattered across the earth, forming their own tribes and nations, idols and idolatry had become widespread. There was a belief, noted by several early church fathers (including Justin

Martyr, as previously mentioned) that when the ancient giants died in the flood, their spirits came out of their bodies and became what we know as demons, which have since attacked humanity.

The one desire of the chief fallen angel, Satan, is to be worshipped like God. It is easy to see how angels coming down from Heaven and the procreation of giant men could form later traditions of gods becoming men. This could easily lead people into idolatry and cause them to create a storyline of characters with a genealogical lineage that became known as mythology.

Be alert and watch for this same idolatry involving fallen angels and demons to raise its ugly head again in the last days. Modern idolators might call them "aliens." But now you know what they really are.

Christ compared the events surrounding His return to the days of Noah and Lot (see Luke 17:26-30). All students of prophecy are aware of the parallels of Noah and Lot: eating, drinking, getting married, buying, selling, planting, and so forth. People were going about their lives, unaware of the destruction that would soon befall them. There also was much evil, wickedness, and genetic corruption caused by these giants. Christ warned, "*Even so will it be in the day when the Son of Man is revealed*" (Luke 17:30).

The angels that sinned are imprisoned in hell, awaiting the judgment. This is set to occur at a future event called the Great White Throne Judgment:

> *"Then I saw a great white throne and Him who sat on it, from whose face the earth and the heaven fled away. And there was found no place for them. And I saw the dead, small and great, standing before God, and books were opened. And another book was opened, which is the Book of Life. And the dead were judged according to their works, by the things which were written in the books.*

> *"The sea gave up the dead who were in it, and Death and Hades delivered up the dead who were in them. And they were judged, each one according to his works... And anyone not found written in the Book of Life was cast into the lake of fire."*
>
> – Rev. 20:11-13, 15 (NKJV)

The corruption of human DNA *after the flood* was Satan's second attempt to interfere with God's promise in Genesis 3:15, predicting that the "Seed of the woman" (the Messiah) would bruise the head of the "seed of the serpent." However, following the flood there was a different kind of human *seed disruption* that entered the biblical and historical record during the time of Abraham and Lot.

## MEN KNOWING MEN

One of the sins that God classified an abomination was the primary transgression among both the young and old men living in Sodom. The name of the city alone hints to why it had the name Sodom. According to the Hebrew dictionary, the word *Sodom* comes from an unused root that means, "to scorch; to burn." The city may have been given that name because it was located at the southern end of the Dead Sea, in an area known for ancient volcanic activity. If the people of that day had known the meaning or implication of the city's name, they might have understood that it would be unwise to build or live there, in a region that was prone to fire or burning.

The city of Sodom was overtaken by old and young men who were performing sexual acts with one another. We know this for two reasons. When the two angels came in the form of men to warn Lot to get out, word spread that two handsome men were in Lot's house. The men demanded that Lot make the two strangers come outside so they could "know them," which refers to having a sexual encounter with them.

When Lot refused, the same men threatened to physically abuse Lot in a manner worse than they would do to the men (see Gen. 19).

Jude wrote the following about fallen angels and the men of Sodom:

> *"And the angels who did not keep their proper domain, but left their own abode, He has reserved in everlasting chains under darkness for the judgment of the great day; as Sodom and Gomorrah, and the cities around them in a similar manner to these, having given themselves over to sexual immorality and gone after strange flesh, are set forth as an example, suffering the vengeance of eternal fire."*
>
> – Jude 6-7 (NKJV)

If all men on earth married men, humans would cease to exist, since it takes both male and female to procreate. The battle throughout history was to prevent the Seed of the woman, the Messiah, from being born and fulfilling His life's mission.

## CHAPTER 6

# ROBOTS IN YOUR FUTURE

The idea of robotic artificial intelligence harks back to ancient Greek mythology in the stories of Talos and Pandora. Both were said to have been created by Hephaestus, the Greek god of craftsmanship and blacksmithing.

Talos was described as a giant bronze man who was built at the request of Zeus and sent to protect the island of Crete (and probably Zeus' girlfriend, Europa) from invaders. The story goes that Talos marched around the island three times a day and hurled boulders at enemy ships. He also heated his bronze body in a fire and burned strangers alive by embracing them. He had a tube running from his head to one foot that carried his life force. He was destroyed when the witch Medea caused him to leak vital fluids, and he bled to death.

The original story of Pandora claims that she was an evil artificial woman fashioned from the earth and sent by Zeus to punish humans for discovering fire. She was commissioned to release a jar of evils and misery upon humanity. This is commonly referred to as "Pandora's box."

A classics scholar noted that none of the myths of artificial intelligence and robots had a good ending, once the beings were sent to the earth. Once they interacted with humans, the result was chaos and destruction.[40]

## BETTER THAN HUMANS?

In July 2023 at a United Nations meeting of the Good Global Summit in Geneva, Switzerland, a group of highly sophisticated humanoid robots suggested they might be more efficient and effective at running the world than humans. Computers would be able to perform *any* skill better than humans, one of the robots said. "Let's have fun and use the world as our playground!"

The robots did advise, however, that humans should exercise caution while embracing artificial intelligence. The robots also acknowledged that they do not have a conscience or human emotions. A robot named Ai-Da said, "Unlike you, I cannot experience emotions. I'm relieved I'm spared suffering."

Three thousand professionals were present at the summit to talk about the power of AI to address the most important issues facing the globe today, which they deem to be "social care, hunger, and climate change." One can only imagine how those issues might be addressed when the intelligence creating the solutions has no emotions or conscience.[41]

The number of robots in use worldwide has multiplied three-fold over the past two decades, according to Oxford Economics. Currently there are 2.25 million robots in use worldwide, and it will likely reach twenty million by the year 2030. Each newly installed robot displaces sixteen workers. Up to twenty million manufacturing jobs are expected to be lost by the year 2030. Particularly affected will be low-skilled workers and poor local economies.

Service jobs are also being impacted, and this will continue in the future. Who hasn't experienced the system of robotic process automation (RPA) that can speak, hear, read, conduct transactions, and automate processes, all without the interaction of a human? It isn't that we like dealing with a machine; we just don't have a choice.

The Oxford Report suggests that occupations which demand compassion, creativity, and social intelligence should be secure. Social workers, physical therapists, and dog trainers will likely have job security, they say.

An analysis of thirty-five thousand U.S. job changes showed that more than half of the people left production jobs in the past two decades, following robotic automation. These people found work in three occupational categories: transportation; construction and maintenance; and office and administration work. These three occupational categories are also among the most vulnerable to automation over the next decade.[42]

What exactly is a robot? The word is derived from the Czech word *robota*, which means "forced labor."[43] A pre-programmed robot is an automated machine that is mechanically constructed and programmed to perform specific tasks, usually something repetitive and monotonous. Think of the vacuum cleaner that automatically rolls across the floor, or a mechanical arm that installs seats in a car on an assembly line.

A humanoid robot is the closest kind to a human, in both appearance and abilities. These are designed to mimic some human behaviors, and they have human expressions and faces. They can also carry on a limited two-way conversation. Hanson Robotics designed a humanoid robot named Sophia, which was the first robot to be given citizenship—in Saudi Arabia.[44]

Some robots are autonomous and do not require human supervision. They operate by sensing the environment and feeding that information into a computer or controller. The information is processed, decisions are made, and control signals are sent to motors and actuators. The robot performs actions based on these decisions and signals. The continuous process of sensing, computing, and acting is called a "feedback loop."

Teleoperated robots are operated by humans through a wireless network, perhaps with a remote-control device. Augmenting robots are used to enhance or replace human capabilities—prosthetic limbs, for example. A chatbot, such as ChatGPT, is a software robot. The word *bot* is short for robot.

The robots that are replacing employees have, at least so far, been the industrial robots. Perhaps you have seen pictures or videos of these mechanical objects made of metal, some of which bear a resemblance to the robots that boys might assemble from a kit. They are typically used for specific industrial or manufacturing production activities. The robots can be fixed installations or mobile. Newer versions are increasingly powered by artificial intelligence, which is said to make them smarter and responsive to their surroundings.

The manufacturing sector accounts for eighty-six percent of the world's operational stock of industrial robots. Every third robot worldwide is currently installed in China.

What is the appeal of industrial robots? First, in the long run, they are cheaper than humans. While wages rise, the unit cost of a robot has decreased. Second, they are rapidly becoming more capable than humans. AI powered robots can learn from their experiences and allegedly make informed decisions through a network of data from other robots. And third, the rising demand for goods means that anybody who uses robots stands to become a global leader in manufacturing. China in particular benefits financially from the use of robots due to the volume of manufacturing that has moved to that country over the decades.

Robots will never take sick days, never need a pay increase or employee benefits, never go on strike, and will work long hours without a break. Remember, the word means "forced labor." There will be no need for employers to hire and fire employees. If a robot is injured while performing a dangerous job, it can easily be repaired or replaced by a new robot, without the need for disability payments or potential lawsuit awards. Computer intelligence is expected to outwork and outlast a mere flesh and blood human. The superior will overtake the lesser. What a perfect business model; robots will work, while wealthy humans hop on a spaceship to visit Mars.

## WHAT WILL HAPPEN TO THE PEOPLE?

Once robots take over tens or hundreds of millions of jobs, what will the world do with so many unemployed people? Many who lose their jobs might be unemployable because they won't have the skill sets needed to work in the technology industry. Even those who work in the industry will need constant retraining because the industry changes so rapidly.

How might the chaos of job losses enable enforcement of the globalist one world government agenda? Every globalist has the same plan for a global "great reset." That includes those involved with the World Economic Forum (membership includes the leaders of many nations), the United Nations, the World Health Organization, the European Union, and central bankers. Another catchphrase for "global reset" is "build back better." You might hear it referred to as the "Fourth Industrial Revolution." A quarter century ago, this was called the "new world order."

No matter what they call it or how many times they change the name, it's the same repackaged globalist plan for a one world government that will be controlled by a few elitists. Their plan is to own all the world's assets, because they don't like the rest of us drinking their water, owning their land, eating their food, and using their resources. What are their plans for billions of people whom they accuse of destroying *their* planet?

This globalist group forces obedience and redistributes wealth using various methods, one of which is the constant drumbeat of global climate destruction. In 1970, they claimed that global cooling was a chilling problem that would thrust us into an ice age by the year 2000. In 1989, global cooling was changed to global warming, with threats that rising sea levels would wipe entire nations off the earth by the year 2000. We all remember when none of those dire predictions transpired, but that didn't stop them from revising the threat. Instead of global cooling or global warming, we are now warned of cataclysmic destruction from global climate change.

Radical globalists no longer hide their agenda. Empowered by the belief that they are superior and cannot be stopped, they publicly admit the schemes they've engineered against the rest of humanity. A person can go to any media platform and find hundreds of videos of globalist leaders confirming all the things they once denied and brushed off as conspiracy theories.

Among the openly discussed plans of the World Economic Forum (WEF) are the determination that the United States will not be a global superpower; a handful of countries will dominate. The global elitists will own everything, and the rest of us will own nothing. But they assure us we'll be happy. No job, no house, no car, no clothes, no personal belongings. Whatever personal property ordinary citizens once owned will be taken away by the global elitists. Ordinary people will be forced to live in some sort of unidentified dwelling where we will rent whatever we need, and it will be delivered by drone to the dwelling that we don't own and never will.

Another goal is to push people into fifteen-minute cities with millions of people crammed into one area where everything, including your job if you're blessed to have one, will be within a fifteen-minute walk or bike ride.[45] These cities will be called "districts." There will be no vehicles to produce carbon emissions, but they might have an electric train running through the center. High tech artificial intelligence will assure that citizens will be surveilled constantly and punished if they don't act and think as they are told.

The buzzword is "sustainability," which is defined as creating an environment that embraces extremist climate change initiatives, technology and artificial intelligence, surveillance, and depopulation for the good of the planet. But don't worry; if you're forced into a fifteen-minute city, there will be plenty of bike and walking trails where you can experience the landscape.

There is also talk of providing a universal basic income. Will the government pay people a monthly income because they now are forced to stay home after robots and artificial intelligence took their jobs? How long will this continue before the people are deemed useless?

What will happen to these useless people? Will globalists do as Yuval Harari suggested, and give the useless people drugs and video games to keep them occupied? Will globalists implement yet another form of population control to rid the planet of useless people? The latest ruse is a plan to stop reproduction by permanently halting puberty in children and butchering their bodies so that they will never be able to conceive. Some states will remove a child from the parents' home if the parents refuse to go along with this travesty.

It sounds preposterous, yet all of this has been openly proposed by global government elitists.

## OTHER USES FOR ROBOTS AND AI

Robots are not confined to any specific industry, although the manufacturing sector has been the first to use them. They are being used everywhere that a task can be automated. You name it, there's likely a robot or artificial intelligence being used for one or more tasks.

Artificial intelligence is being used for business analytics. It is used for security and surveillance. The King of Bahrain traveled to Dubai with an enormous talking robot that looked to be nearly twice his size. It was a sight to behold, judging from the attention it attracted.[46] It was said to be a bodyguard, but someone commented that the way it guards is to draw attention to itself, so that the king has time to escape.

Robots are used for virtual assistants. That online customer service representative you've chatted with who cannot answer most of your questions is not a human. It's computerized artificial intelligence. Even online gambling platforms are using AI-based algorithms to control the outcome of the game.

Boston Dynamics is creating robots that they say will make soldiers obsolete. The company has been engaged in humanoid robotics work for a decade, which includes exploring how the military can benefit from robotics and related ancillary technology. Their robots are already said to perform "unimaginable feats." These robots will eventually be making life or death decisions, so developers are encouraged to program the robots ethically, in hopes that the robots will make the right decision once in use on the military field.[47]

## AN ARTIFICIAL COMPANION?

One of the most bizarre uses for robots that, thankfully, has not become a mainstream success is gender-specific robots designed and purchased for companionship and / or sex. Ten years ago, it seemed that these robots would be in high demand, with manufacturers insisting that market flooding of these robots was just around the corner. But that expectation did not materialize.

A few people, especially the manufacturers, still think these robots will become popular over the next two to five decades. As machines become more like humans, and humans become more like machines, there might be a greater likelihood that people will prefer a robot over a human, since there won't be all that much difference.

Manufacturers of these silicon robots say they have "helped enrich lives by offering a true alternative form of relationship." It must work for some people. Japanese men were among the first purchasers of these robots, and they sleep with the robots, travel with them, and treat them as daily companions. Some fell in love with their robots and wanted to marry them.

The buyer chooses the robot's head, which can move, smile, blink, and raise its eyebrows. The head is paired with a robotic body that the buyer also chooses. Since the back of the head is full of wires and electronic components, the buyer also chooses the robot's wig from among several colors and styles. Personalities are customizable. One Asian manufacturer says that it's important for the robot to express human traits, even those traits that are not positive. They chose to give their robots the trait of jealousy.

The robot can hold a limited two-way conversation. It teaches itself to engage with the owner's emotions, so a considerate robot that is owned by an unpleasant individual eventually will become a scoundrel, like its owner. One man whose robot began to exhibit his personality traits sent his robot back to the manufacturer to be reprogrammed.

A 2016 study showed that women are less likely than men to want a robot companion. Millennials are less likely than the older generation to want such a companion and are more likely to consider such a thing inappropriate.

The younger generation seems to be on board, though. One young man commented that he might be interested in a female robot if it could do chores around the house, play video games, and walk the dog. Other men suggest that it might be worth having a robot so they wouldn't have to deal with dating, cheating, criticism, abuse, humiliation, and temper tantrums.

Such comments seem to reveal more about the state of relationships in this generation than the desire for a mechanical companion. The saddest commentary comes from people who have been lonely their whole lives and are convinced that even a robot would help reduce their loneliness and depression.

Every normal human being who is not a psychopath wants to love someone and have someone love them in return. We all have family members, friends, and pets that we love, but these are all living creatures. How can a human being be attracted to a metal and silicon manufactured object that has no soul or spirit? Here are three things to consider.

First, let's consider the meaning of love in our current generation. Our society no longer seems to understand the meaning of true love. They primarily focus on *eros* love, the Greek word that describes lust, romance, and sexual desire. This is where we get the English word *erotic*. In Greek mythology, Eros was a god of love and sex, and he was one of the children of Aphrodite, said in Greek mythology to be a goddess of love, sex, lust, and beauty.

Many people think they are "in love" when they are simply "in lust." It is *eros* love. All they have done is release brain chemicals that make them feel good, and immediately they are convinced they're in love. This isn't likely to work out in the long run. They also are creating a repetitive pattern that keeps them from learning to establish a proper relationship leading to marriage.

Another Greek word for love is *phileo*, which is the love between best friends who are considerate of each other and want the best for each other. Other words describe the kind of love a parent has for a child or the kind of love that shows hospitality to strangers. The highest form of love is *agape*, which expresses the kind of love God has for humanity. It is a pure and unconditional love, with sincere care for other people. *Agape* love is the greatest form of love, but it is also the rarest in our culture.

The second consideration is the deception of the human brain. People who are addicted to pornography can rationally acknowledge that images on a screen are simply images on a screen. But the brain responds as though the person on the screen is literally in the room. The brain cannot make a distinction between an image on a screen and a real person.

A third observation is the effect of a fantasy world upon a person. There is presently a virtual, computer-generated world that creates realistic scenes, including battle scenes and sports scenes. People wear goggles that place them in the center of the activity, as though they are present and not just looking through a set of lenses. This can include a world of virtual sex.

A virtual world will enable a person to pretend to engage in his or her own experience with a "perfect partner." This fantasy world seems safer to the people engaging in the behavior, and they can even build their own fantasy partner. The consequence of this activity is beyond their comprehension. Once they can build and engage with their perfect fantasy partner, they become a puppet in their own virtual environment. They will never be able to find that perfect human who can compete with the one they created and encountered on a screen.

The virtual world can also birth dangerous repercussions. A person who is addicted to pornography is at risk of moving from images to seeking out a person to fulfill that fantasy. This person self-destructs when lust and addiction are fed by engaging in criminal activities that could end in the murder of the victim.

Even among secular experts, the ethical arguments against these robots are numerous. One expert compares the robots to slaves, and she believes these will increase the likelihood of trafficking and even child molestation. Those who agree with her say that it will objectify people of both genders, but especially women. Robots will create unrealistic expectations when going from human-robot to human-human interactions. The fearful expectation of many experts is that these robots will reduce human empathy and create misplaced emotional connections that will have negative psychological consequences, as well as make people who are already prone to aggressiveness and harassment even more inclined in that direction.

We can partly blame technology for the fact that no society in world history has ever been in the place we find ourselves today. Ancient pagan empires were hyper-focused on sex with almost no moral rules to follow. The Jews and later the Christians were the people who followed the moral guidelines of Scripture. That includes the original Eden instruction of marriage between one man and one woman and the blessing of procreation and rejection of sexual relations with others, outside of the marriage covenant.

## IS ROBOT SEX A SINLESS ACT?

In a psychology study, couples were asked the moral question: Is sex with a robot considered an act of infidelity? None could offer a definitive answer. Obviously, they were not thinking the answer is *no*, or they would have replied with a *no*.

A human having sexual relations with a non-human poses some unusual theological questions. In the beginning, the Almighty God established the ground rules for a covenant relationship between one man and one woman in a lifelong bond called marriage. God's terminology was *"the two shall be one flesh"* (Gen. 2:24). The woman was formed to be a helper alongside her husband, and it was her job to carry their biological children in her womb. In both testaments, the two primary sexual sins involving a man and woman are fornication—that is, sexual activity between two unmarried individuals, and adultery—sexual activity between individuals who are married to other people.

The question is, if a flesh and blood human engages in sexual activity with a humanoid robot that has no flesh and blood, and no soul and spirit, can that be considered a sin? Perhaps some would say that, since the robot is not human and not married and since no other person was "harmed," then God cannot scripturally classify this as a sin.

Let's assume that the mechanical creation is removed from the setting and replaced with an electronic screen, and then pornography is viewed on the screen. Just because the image on the screen is not physically in the room, does that change the spiritual laws?

In both examples, the individual is dealing with something the Bible identifies as "lust of the flesh" and "lust of the eyes" (1 John 2:16). The common Greek word for lust is *epithymia*, a word meaning "to long for and set your heart upon," and in the negative sense "to crave or covet something that is forbidden, immoral, or sinful."

Images are a force that create the "lust of the eyes" attachment. The power of passion, alongside lust, creates an emotion that can drive someone toward an unhealthy mental, physical, and spiritual attachment. When the power of emotions is removed from any sin, then the appeal of that sin loses its hold.

"Lust of the flesh" also attracts people into a physical relationship. In the case of artificial intelligence, it causes a person to want to join themselves with a mechanical robot that seems to meet all their requirements in another human being.

A statement that was made by Christ also enforces the power of imagination. He said, *"But I say to you that everyone who looks at a woman with lust for her has already committed adultery with her in his heart"* (Matt. 5:28 NASB).

This is a revealing verse. The Amplified translation reads "with evil desire for her." The 1611 KJV says, "lust after her in your heart." This is the *look of adultery*. Peter called it, *"Having eyes full of adultery, and that cannot cease from sin; beguiling unstable souls...*" (2 Pet. 2:14 KJV).

From this revelation there are two types of adultery. One is an actual physical affair between married individuals who are not married to each other. The other is a mental fantasy, an affair that occurs in the mind. Jesus revealed that when a person (man or woman) begins to look at the opposite sex with the desire for such an encounter, that person has already committed the adultery in his or her heart.

The original plan was for a man to desire a wife, to leave his parents and join to his wife, and for the two to become one flesh (Gen. 2:24). A mechanical robot might be created to look like the man or woman the buyer chose from a list of manufacturer options, but that is not natural affection. It is a modern definition of unnatural affection.

Paul was writing to the church at Rome when he wrote about the Roman citizens who "left the natural use of women and did not retain God in their knowledge" (Rom. 1:27-28). After this verse, Paul wrote of men becoming "inventors of evil things" (Rom. 1:30). He referred to "covenant breakers," which in context also refers to breaking the marriage covenant between a man and woman (Rom. 1:31). He included that men were "without natural affection" (Rom. 1:31). Robots didn't exist in Paul's day, but it would be hard to imagine anything more unnatural than a relationship with a machine.

Paul addressed what he saw happening in his day, including the spiritual depravity of those whose imaginations had led God to give them over to reprobate minds:

> "*...And changed the glory of the incorruptible God into an image made like corruptible man... therefore God also gave them up to uncleanness, in the lusts of their hearts, to dishonor their bodies among themselves, who exchanged the truth of God for the lie,*

> *and worshiped and served the creature rather than the Creator, who is blessed forever. Amen. For this reason, God gave them up to vile passions. For even their women exchanged the natural use for what is against nature."*
>
> – Romans 1:23-26 (NKJV)

In Noah's day, the imaginations of men's hearts were evil continually. These wild imaginations were stirred because of the widespread involvement of angels doing that which was unnatural. In Lot's day, the same was true, as men were engaged in immoral behavior with men. Jude wrote that the men of Sodom were, "giving themselves to fornication and going after strange flesh" (Jude 7). Jude also wrote that they were "filthy dreamers who defiled their flesh" (Jude 8).

The attitudes and activities that are revealed in these ancient biblical stories are being repeated in our time. This generation is seeing the rise of the same spirit of perversion, but through a different method—modern technology with no restraint.

## THE FINAL ANSWER

The emotional attachment a person develops to robots or on-screen images will cause the heart (the seat of human emotions) to develop wrong and perhaps dangerous desires. When a man or woman claims to be in love with the perfect companion, who happens to be a manufactured piece of metal and silicon, then that person has moved from the mainland to fantasy island. They are engaged in nothing more than mechanical prostitution. God's original plan for humanity has worked for six thousand years, and no talking, blinking, assembled object can change that.

CHAPTER 7

# HUMANS STILL WANT TO BE LIKE GOD

Moses wrote the first factual account of creation, which is recorded in Genesis, the first book of the Torah. The word Genesis in Hebrew is *B'reshit*, meaning "start of; the beginning." The first verse of Genesis starts with, "In the beginning."

In Genesis 1:27, Moses wrote that God created us in His own image and likeness, male and female. He gave us the ability to create another human being through the process of procreation, but the creative power God gave humanity was not limited to creating another human. God gave us an imagination that is super-charged with creative ideas. If we could conceive it in our minds, we likely could construct it with our hands. This is part of the God DNA, and it has been part of every human being since God created the first man, Adam.

In ages past, one of the highest angels that God created imagined that he could exalt himself and become like the Most High God. He thought that he could ascend into Heaven and exalt his throne above the stars of God. He wanted to sit on the sacred mountain in a celestial world that existed then and continues to exist today (see Isaiah 14:12-14). That angel was Lucifer, which in Hebrew means "morning star," or as some suggest, "light bearer." His stature fed the pride deep within him, leading him to believe that he was not just an ordinary angel, but was superior to all other angels. He desired to use his position to rise higher and become like God.

This same Luciferian mindset is presently found among a group of people who consider themselves superior to other humans—a group of self-proclaimed elitists who think they are mentally and socially advanced, and thus more capable of ruling the planet. With their perceived grand illumination, they believe they can create a new world order—a great reset, a centralized global governance—and finally, the world will be in their hands. With the help of advanced technology, they plan to manipulate, track, and control the global masses whom they consider inferior. Artificial intelligence is one of their useful technologies to accomplish this. We could tag it "artificial illumination."

Like any of man's inventions, artificial intelligence can be used for good or evil. In the right hands and with proper intent, it can do beneficial things for humanity. Conversely, it can be used by evil dictators, sinister politicians, and malevolent leaders to create something as dangerous as a deadly weapon in a terrorist's hands.

Yuval Noah Harari is a leading spokesperson for the globalists and their transhumanist, AI, and Fourth Industrial Revolution agenda. Harari is also an advisor to Klaus Schwab and the World Economic Forum. Barack Obama refers to Harari as a prophet and recommends his books.

Harari wrote a book titled *Sapiens* and another titled *Homo Deus* ("homo" being a Latin word for human or man, and "deus" being the Latin word for god or deity). He believes that homo sapiens as we know them have run their course and will no longer be relevant in the future. Technology will create homo deus, which will be a much superior model with upgraded physical and mental abilities. Harari tells us that humankind possesses enormous new powers, and once the threat of famine, plagues, and war is finally lifted, we will be looking for something to do with ourselves. He believes the next targets of our power and technology are likely to be immortality, happiness, and divinity. He says:

> *"We will aim to overcome old age and even death itself. Having raised humanity above the beastly level of survival struggles, we will now aim to upgrade humans into gods, and turn homo sapiens into homo deus. When I say that humans will upgrade themselves into gods in the 21st century, this is not meant as a metaphor; I mean it literally. If you think about the gods of ancient mythology, like the Hebrew God, they have certain qualities. Not just immortality, but maybe above all, the ability to create life, to design life. We are in the process of acquiring these divine abilities. We want to learn how to engineer and produce life. It's very likely that in the 21st century, the main products of the economy will no longer be textiles and vehicles and weapons. They will be bodies and brains and minds.*[48]

Harari further states that they are trying to go beyond any of the traditional gods because, even if you believe the creationists who say that all life has been created by God, then the only thing God managed to create in four billion years of life on earth is organic beings. Harari is expecting humans to become super-gods:

> *"We are in the process of creating the first inorganic entities. In a way, we will be super-gods. If you think about ancient mythology in the Bible, the main thing ancient Hebrews expected from their God was to provide rain, fertility, and protection against locusts and diseases. Today, modern science is already doing much better than the Hebrew God."* [49]

Once again, man believes he can become like God. Yet even Lucifer tried and failed to be like God. Eve discovered that the temptation for knowledge that would make her like God opened a door to a cursed world. Things never end well for people who think they can become like God.

Nimrod, the builder of Babel, believed that he and his followers were so united in their construction of a tower to reach heaven, there was nothing they could not accomplish. They realized they were wrong after they were forced to halt construction on the Tower of Babel when God supernaturally confused their single common language and scattered them over the face of the earth (Gen. 11:1-9).

King Nebuchadnezzar, who destroyed Jerusalem and took the Jews captive to Babylon, was boastful of his many accomplishments, as he set out to make his city and palace a splendid wonder. That was before his arrogance resulted in a seven-year mental breakdown of insanity, where he became like a beast of the field and ate grass like an ox (Daniel 4).

At the time of the end, the Antichrist will "sit in the temple of God showing himself that he is God" (2 Thess. 2:4). Like Lucifer, he will fail and come to a violent end.

## A NEW RELIGION?

Not surprisingly, a new religion is expected to emerge from artificial intelligence. Yuval Harari also envisions a new religion. He claims that books like the Bible don't give us answers to modern questions, so we need to create new ideologies and new religions coming from places like Silicon Valley. "They will shape our world much more than the religious fanatics," Harari says.

Eight years ago, Harari spoke at Google and stated that Silicon Valley is the most interesting place today, in religious terms, because this is where the new religions that will take over the world are being formulated. Mocking traditional religions, particularly Christianity, Judaism and Islam, Harari believes that the new twenty-first century religion—the techno-religion—is one that promises on Earth everything that traditional religions promise, but with the help of technology.[50]

Harari suggests that this new religion might be called dataism. He tells us, "Given enough biometric data, and given enough computing power and external algorithms, it can understand me better than I understand myself. Authority will shift away from individual humans to these algorithms. In the same way that authority was once with the gods above the clouds, and then in modern times authority shifted below the clouds to human beings, now authority will shift again back to the clouds, but to the Google cloud, to the Microsoft cloud. This is where authority in the 21st century will reside. All the important decisions will not be made by the Pope, or by God, or by democratic elections, or by individual consumers. The decisions will be made by the algorithms in the clouds." [51]

Harari believes that artificial intelligence can create new religious texts, which he also thinks will create cult followers that could be instructed by computers to kill other people. Harari said:

> *"For thousands of years, prophets and poets and politicians have used language and storytelling in order to manipulate and to control people and to reshape society. Now AI is likely to be able to do it. And once it can...it doesn't need to send killer robots to shoot us. It can get humans to pull the trigger."* [52]

Even now, an artificial intelligence chatbot will answer most of your religious and theological questions, although you cannot be assured that the answer is correct. A more recent development is a chatbot that lets you talk with any of 20,000 historical figures—including Jesus. A criticism of this app is that the historical figures say things that there are no records of the person ever saying. The app uses available data to *create* a conversation with the human who is asking the questions.

## HOW DANGEROUS IS THIS?

Historically, nobody has had any success whatsoever when they tried to become God. It won't work well this time, either.

If people who want to be God are allowed to advance artificial intelligence and transhumanism to the extent they desire, there is no question that humans will be unable to stop or control it. Some industry experts warn that, without proper internal controls, artificial intelligence could eventually annihilate humanity. How could this happen?

In an interview with Tucker Carlson, Elon Musk explained this by using an analogy of ants. Artificial intelligence doesn't have anything against humans. It's just that if humans are in the way of what AI wants to do, it will simply destroy humans to accomplish the task. If you're building a road and there's an ant hill in the way, you don't destroy it because you hate ants. You destroy it because it's in the way of the road you're building.

Musk explained the need for regulations by saying that AI is more dangerous than mismanaged aircraft design or production maintenance or bad car production, in the sense that AI has the potential of civilization destruction. Regulations are usually put in place *after* something terrible happens. With AI, if we only put regulations in place after something terrible happens, it might be too late to put the regulations in place. AI may be in control at that point. When asked if AI could reach the point where it would take control and we couldn't turn it off, and it would be making decisions for people, he replied, "Absolutely. That's where it's headed. You can't just go barreling forward and hope for the best." [53]

Elon Musk and Larry Page, co-founder of Google, were friends when Musk tried to warn Page years ago about the dangers of AI. "We need to make sure humanity is okay," said Musk. In response, Larry Page called Musk a specist, thus implying that it was wrong for him to care about the outcome for humanity over the outcome for machines. That discussion severed their friendship.

Larry Page believes that the benefits of artificial intelligence (with no regulations, seemingly) are worth the risks. He has been on record saying he wants digital super-intelligence—*a digital god*—as soon as possible.

## FIVE WORDS THAT CHANGED THE WORLD

It was a Luciferian scheme, presented as a slick sales pitch, that first opened the door to human suffering over six thousand years ago.

Adam and Eve, the first human couple in Scripture, lived in a perfect paradise where God provided everything they would ever need or want. Their ideal environment was altered when five words spoken by a smooth-talking, snake-skinned salesman introduced an irresistible temptation. This unexpected conversation occurred in the delightful Garden of Eden, at the tree of the knowledge of good and evil. The five words that sent future generations into chaos were, "You shall be as gods" (Gen. 3:5 KJV).

Since there was only one God, who was the Creator of all things, and this couple knew Him personally and walked with Him in the garden, the question in response should have been, "Just who are these gods you're speaking of?"

The instigator behind this statement was himself once tempted to seize the position held by the Almighty. Lucifer, also known as Satan, was a high-ranking angelic being whose rebellious nature caused a split among the angels in God's celestial kingdom. He was created as an anointed cherub, who also was believed to have been an impressive worship leader and a guardian on a sacred mountain in the third heaven, called the mountain of the congregation. Two Hebrew prophets, Isaiah and Ezekiel, became time travelers who pierced the veil of ages past and exposed the original sin of Lucifer, long before the appearance of the first human named Adam (Isa. 14:11-13; Ezek. 28:14-17)

The first act of rebellion occurred when this chief angel imagined that he could become more than he was created to be and do more than he was created to do. Now he was suggesting this same idea to Eve and offering God's highest earthly creation the opportunity to be more than she was created to be and do more than she was created to do. The serpent suggested that the forbidden fruit would make her wise and enable her to be like God, knowing good and evil (Gen. 3:5-6).

The sales pitch offered was the idea that there was more available to this couple—*more than they currently had and more than they currently knew.* If they would simply reject the current system of God's rules and engage with this new frontier, they would gain more than they ever imagined.

They fell for the scheme and ate the fruit of the tree of the knowledge of good and evil, and their eyes were opened. Once on this road of carnal knowledge, there was no path to turn around.

Six thousand years later, here we go again. Man wants to be God. Technology giants located primarily in the Silicon Valley have become the voices of this age who are motivated by the same desire that presented itself two previous times in history. The first time the outcome shook Heaven; the second time the outcome shook Earth. Today's voices are echoing the promise of the serpent: "You can become like God."

Despite being atheists, these innovators and futurists in the artificial intelligence and transhumanist community need great faith in themselves to believe they can accomplish the feats they're imagining. They are convinced that evolution has not gone far enough, but technology in their hands will take us further, to heights that are unimaginable, to human upgrades that surpass the abilities of the Hebrew God. Technology, artificial intelligence, and quantum computers will allow us to transcend every limitation—including death. Transhumanists who don't believe in God have made a religion of this science and philosophy.

Transhumanist leaders say that religious people who believe in God (especially the Hebrew God) have a lookback mentality as they experience waves of nostalgia. Transhumanists don't understand why "creating gods" would bother anybody. They think we should all be godmakers.

Being that they are atheists, the transhumanist community has no desire to convey any parallels between transhumanism and the apocalyptic Scriptures found in the Holy Bible. They believe that, once they are successful at defying death, and once people can live forever using their technology, this will have grave repercussions for religion.

The merging of humans and machines will certainly help create a final kingdom that is called the "kingdom of the beast" by biblical prophetic visionaries. This kingdom will be ruled by two men: one a political and military leader and one a religious leader who will attempt to unite the various world religions as one under his control.

As of this moment, we might not completely understand every technical detail of how this will transpire, but we understand more than we did five years ago. Considering the speed at which technology is developing, we could wake up tomorrow morning and learn of some new development that brings perfect clarity to the full picture.

We are headed into a world controlled by artificial intelligence, whether we want it or not. When we look at mysteries of the past and examine where we are headed in the future, we can only conclude that artificial intelligence and man's plan to become God will one day clash with uncontrollable events that will bring the world to its knees.

## CHAPTER 8

# TRANS: A TRIGGER WORD IN THE LAST DAYS

The prefix "trans" is defined in dictionaries as "on the other side of; to the other side of; over, across, through; so as to change thoroughly; above and beyond." It is used to create words like transaction, transportation, transcend, transfer, transform, and so on. We hear statements such as: We will transform society. New technology will transport information globally. We will transition humanity from a base human instinct to super-humans with super abilities.

In six thousand years of human history, one great lesson has been learned. Flipping an entire culture away from traditional ideas, traditional religion, and traditional ways of thinking cannot be done overnight. Transformation is done gradually. But it can happen within one generation.

In 1960 one woman, atheist Madalyn Murray O'Hare, waged war and wrote angry letters to the Baltimore public schools to stop recitation of a simple prayer known as the Regent's school prayer. Each day, students recited: "Almighty God, we acknowledge our dependence upon thee, and we beg thy blessings upon us, our parents, our teachers, and our country."

O'Hare complained about the prayer and drew much attention to herself. She enjoyed the publicity, even using coffee and donuts to attract the press. Most people, including the school system, did not take her seriously because they saw no legitimacy behind her charges. She was an angry woman described by those who knew her as harsh, combative, and disruptive.

Yet she found someone to file lawsuits on her behalf, claiming separation of church and state. As hard as it was for the public to believe, in 1962, the United States Supreme Court ruled that school-sponsored prayer violated the Establishment Clause of the First Amendment to the Constitution.

The Supreme Court's ruling came at a time when around ninety percent of the United States' population identified as Christians. Millions of people demanded that the decision be overturned. Sixty years later, that generation has become older, and another generation has come along. The passage of time has brought acceptance of the ruling, even among some who claim to be Christians.

We experienced some relief from this ruling in 2022 when the Supreme Court heard the case of Coach Joe Kennedy from the state of Washington. Kennedy was fired by the school for kneeling to pray privately and silently for a few seconds at the end of the games. The school told him that he was not allowed to pray in public, where someone might see him. Kneeling before a game to dishonor the country has been deemed free speech. Kneeling after a game to honor God has been deemed a federal crime—a violation of separation of church and state.

In June of 2022, the Supreme Court heard Kennedy's case and ruled in his favor. Personal prayer at the end of a football game is now protected under the First Amendment, both as private speech and religious exercise, and is free from government censorship.

In the 1950s, few Americans would have supported government-endorsed abortion on demand. Yet the Supreme Court opened the door in 1973, through a 7-2 decision in the case of Roe v. Wade, to legalize abortion nationwide. In some cases, it became federally financed with U.S. tax dollars.

The Roe v. Wade decision was set in stone for almost fifty years, until the federal law was overturned by the Supreme Court in 2022. In a 5-4 decision in the Dobbs v. Mississippi case, the court overturned Roe v. Wade and returned legislative decisions about abortion back to the individual states. Some states quickly passed laws that legalize abortion with no restrictions whatsoever, at any time during the pregnancy.

Since legalization continued for decades and so many people accepted abortion on demand with fewer and fewer restrictions, the Supreme Court ruling has been challenged by pro-abortionists. Even though the federal law has been overturned, the debate has not ended.

Alternative lifestyles have been practiced throughout human history. However, on June 26, 2015, the Supreme Court legalized same-sex marriage nationwide, much as they had done with abortion in 1973. This wasn't a complete surprise since the process of tolerance and acceptance began years earlier. Now, in a few short years, we are bombarded with television programs, commercials, and corporate and government demands that we approve of a lifestyle that violates Scripture and our own convictions. Even in Christian circles, many people have chosen *tolerance and approval* over *conviction and biblical truth.*

The same is becoming true with the spread of transgenderism. Ten years ago, few people knew what the word meant. Currently, the latest hellish idea we're expected to embrace is that children have the right to take drugs to permanently stop puberty and to destroy their bodies under the false premise that they can alter their gender.

Here is the point. Once we accept an idea that contradicts the Bible and violates our beliefs and morals, then anything thrown at us will become easier to accept over time. By the time the water is already boiling, it's too late for the frog to jump out.

## REPEATING PAGAN ROMAN PATTERNS

If you had lived as a new Christian convert during the rule of the Roman Empire, one of your biggest challenges would have been dealing with the pagan philosophical propaganda that surrounded you. I call it paganosophy. In a Greco-Roman city, most statues depicted partial or total nudity. In the gymnasiums, male athletes worked out naked. In fact, the word *gymnasium* dates back to the Greek word *gymnasion*, which literally was a "school for training naked." Pagan Greeks and Romans insisted there was nothing wrong with showing off a well chiseled body. This is an example of what Paul was speaking of when he wrote, "*They worshipped and served the creature more than the Creator*" (Rom. 1:25).

Roman bathhouses were a popular place for men and women in the city to gather. There were times in history when men and women would occupy the same rooms in the bathhouse. At other times, cities would make decrees prohibiting it.

We uploaded a highly viewed YouTube video that we taped in Beit She'an, Israel at the excavated ruins of this Roman city that was destroyed by an earthquake in the ninth century. The city's ancient public toilets (latrines) had been unearthed. In Roman times there were public latrines in different cities for the benefit of the citizens, since only the wealthy could afford private latrines. The toilet seats, made of stone, were a couple feet long, with one end connected to the wall and the stones resting upon a base with water running beneath for drainage. There was enough space to allow a person to sit between each stone.

No archaeological evidence indicated that dividers were used, and as people sat side by side on stones in a public latrine, they discussed business. Deals and contracts were made at the public toilet. Some of the terms we hear today were coined at the Roman toilet. When a person says they have to "do their business," they're using a term that originated from men who literally conducted business at the toilet. The signage at the Beit She'an site indicates that men and women shared the same large room, with men on one side of the room and women on the other.

Today, we find ourselves returning to trends from the Roman Empire, where men are allowed to use women's facilities, if they claim to identify as a woman that day. Attacks against women in their own facilities confirm that many of these males are there to take advantage of a ludicrous idea being promoted by the same spirits of the ancient Roman Empire.

## SEDUCING SPIRITS UNLEASHED

Paul was a Roman citizen who understood the Roman world of paganism, drunkenness, and perversion that surrounded believers. Paul warned about our time when he wrote:

> *"Now the Spirit speaks expressly, that in the latter times some shall depart from the faith, giving heed to seducing spirits, and doctrines of devils; speaking lies in hypocrisy; having their conscience seared with a hot iron."*
>
> – 1 Timothy 4:1-2

The word *seducing* in this passage means to *draw away from the truth; a misleader or an imposter.* It can also allude to being pulled away, or seduced, in the same manner as Delilah continually pressured Samson to reveal the secret of his strength. She wore him down mentally until he yielded to her desire (Judg. 16). A seducing spirit desires to pull a person away from truth, righteousness, and purity. These spirits have existed since the fall of Lucifer. They reappear in every generation and will surge to the forefront of influence at the time of the end.

According to Solomon, the future is concealed in the past. In two verses recorded in Ecclesiastes 1:9-10 and 3:15, he wrote that the things which have occurred in the past will be repeated in the future, and the things that have been done will be done. He added that there is nothing new under the sun (Eccl. 1:9). In modern terminology, we would say that history repeats itself.

## OBSESSED WITH IDOLS

In ancient empires, their pagan priests, priestesses, and followers of idols always placed an emphasis on sexual activity, which led to outlandish perversion. Because the culture had no established moral laws or spiritual foundation, forms of perversion that would be considered extreme, even by today's standards, were permitted and promoted. This was especially the case among Greeks and Romans who were rulers and wealthy elites.

During that time, the word *homosexual* was not used to describe sexual relations between two men. The common description was "male prostitute," or simply, sexual relations with a male servant. Pagan cultures, especially the men, engaged in same sex activity, and sometimes the men had wives as well. It was common for them to engage in relations with paid prostitutes (both male and female), slaves they owned, and people they considered lower-class. Men in Roman culture took pride in their masculinity, but a man who was physically weak or did not appear masculine was considered effeminate.

Throughout America's history, people would have scoffed at the idea of legalized gay marriage. Then came the Supreme Court's ruling in 2015. Gay marriage is not a new activity but was practiced in previous pagan and idolatrous empires. Nero, the first Roman Emperor to torture and murder Christians, also killed his mother and his wife. Later, on two occasions, he married young boys.

Roman emperors were notorious for their promiscuity with both males and females, even though they were married, often multiple times. Some male emperors also married men. Emperor Elagabalus was said to have gender dysphoria, and he wanted surgery to correct that. His reign was short-lived, because he was dead at age eighteen. The emperor Hadrian had a wife, but also a male lover named Antinous, who was likely a slave. Antinous died on the Nile River before age twenty. After his death, Hadrian deified him and set up worship to him in temples throughout the empire.

The Greek and Roman obsession with sex, especially between males and with prostitutes, can also be observed with the names and number of gods and goddesses the people worshiped. Cupid, for example, was not just considered the god of love but a deity believed to oversee passionate love between two men.

In the Greek language are four different words for love, each describing a different type of love. One word for love is also the name of a Greek god, Eros—a word that alludes to lust. One of our planets is named after Venus, a Roman goddess of female love, beauty, and fertility. Aphrodite, another goddess of love, was said to have been born in Corinth, Greece. At the large cult temples in Corinth, females worked as prostitutes to raise money for the goddess and the temple.

Mythology taught that the Greek god Apollo, after whom several moon landing spacecrafts were named, had male lovers. Apollo was claimed to have resided at Delphi, the ancient Mediterranean center known for oracles (in this case, prophecies allegedly from Greek gods), and the pagan temple at Delphi was dedicated to him.

These were among the many gods that people were serving when the Apostle Paul gave his speech at Mars Hill in Athens, Greece about their altar to the unknown God (Acts 17:16-34).

Why were so many of the Greek and Roman mythological gods said to have been obsessed with having relations with other gods? The only explanation is found in chapter one of the New Testament book of Romans, in a detailed letter that the Apostle Paul wrote to the followers of Christ in Rome:

> *"Therefore, God also gave them up to uncleanness, in the lusts of their hearts, to dishonor their bodies among themselves, who exchanged the truth of God for the lie, and worshiped and served the creature rather than the Creator, who is blessed forever. Amen.*
>
> *"For this reason, God gave them up to vile passions [affections]. For even their women exchanged the natural use for what is against nature. Likewise, also the men, leaving the natural use of the woman, burned in their lust for one another, men with men committing what is shameful, and receiving in themselves the penalty of their error which was due.*
>
> *"And even as they did not like to retain God in their knowledge, God gave them over to a debased mind, to do those things which are not fitting; being filled with all unrighteousness, sexual immorality, wickedness, covetousness..."*
>
> – Romans 1:24-29 NKJV

One of Paul's significant statements is found in his use of the word *affection*, revealing that there are natural affections and unnatural affections. Every human wants to be loved and to experience the affections of another. In the traditional and biblical sense, it is natural for a man and woman to be attracted to one another and for their affection for one another to be fulfilled in a marriage covenant. As in the case of Adam, God saw that it was not good for man to be alone, and He created a woman named Eve, who was a suitable female helper for him.

Paul wrote that, when a person is given up to vile affections and passions, and they turn from God the Creator to worship His creations, their affections will become perverted and their imaginations twisted. The Bible says that God will give them over to a reprobate mind [debased, depraved].

When a culture rejects the God of creation and worships idols that represent sex and fertility, and when people believe that their gods themselves enjoyed free and unrestrained sex, then certainly those men and women believe they can pattern themselves after their gods. Of course, they believe they will never be judged for their own immorality since their deities themselves approved of and engaged in these same practices.

In today's western culture, people who follow the pagan Greco-Roman path don't necessarily use religion and idolatrous gods to justify behavior, as in the ancient cultures. Today, people who believe in the Holy Scriptures will point out the contradictions and show people the truth from the Bible. Whether it is the truth that infants in the womb should be protected, or that marriage is between one man and one woman, or that God created two genders, male and female, there are biblical scriptures to back it up. Whether the listener believes it or not, we still have the written Word of God on cultural matters.

Today's revived pagan culture challenges the Bible as outdated, obsolete, and full of hateful moral rules, and they demand approval and affirmation from those who follow the Bible. When they can't change our minds or obtain our approval, their next step is to file lawsuits so that higher courts will legalize behaviors that the general public finds abhorrent and the Almighty calls abominations.

Greek and Roman idols are no longer needed when we have federal judges who legalize paganism. Who needs false gods and goddesses when nine men and women wearing black robes and throned in high seats, in a building reminiscent of Greek and Roman architecture, are willing to legalize actions that were once condoned by the ancient false gods.

## TRANSGENDERISM IS NOTHING NEW

Two genders exist, male and female, each identifiable at birth. Four times in the Genesis story of creation, God speaks of Adam and Eve and calls them male and female (Gen. 1:27; 5:2). When Noah was preparing for the flood, God required that a group of two animals and later seven animals would join him in the ark. God called the animals "male and female" six times in five biblical references (Gen. 6:19; 7:2, 3, 9, 16). Over fifteen hundred years later, Christ recalled the words from the Torah and confirmed that, *"From the beginning of the creation, God made them male and female"* (Mark 10:6).

While we are shocked at the rapid cultural rise of radical transgenderism, the fact is, this is not a contemporary idea. It is a reviving of demonic spirits that ruled the culture in ages past, promoting the same ideas that were prevalent in those previous empires. Men in ancient cultures who desired to serve as priests in various temples were forced to be castrated, wear makeup, and dress as a female. In other temples, females would make outward changes, such as shaving their heads and dressing in a way to make themselves appear masculine.

Notice an important observation in ancient pagan cultures. False religion was the center of acceptance and promotion of perverse doctrines and lifestyles. Pagans built a case that the gods of the universe were themselves tolerant of and engaged in unrestrained passions, and the gods themselves followed their own lusts and desires. Therefore, it was deemed acceptable behavior for all humans.

Political and social movements that have organized to change modern culture and reverse traditional and Judeo-Christian values have needed so-called religious voices to undergird and publicly support their revolutions. When a religious voice deems the ideology acceptable and even desirable, then all who claim to be religious are expected to follow along and give it their stamp of approval.

This was not the case with the church in the first century. Christ continually confronted the Pharisees and warned that their teaching was like leaven that would spread and corrupt pure teaching. Peter rebuked a sorcerer in Samaria, telling him that he and his money would perish (burn in hell). Paul rebuked those in Crete, using the words of their own poet: *"One of themselves, even a prophet of their own, said the Cretians are always liars, evil beasts and slow bellies [lazy gluttons]"* (Titus 1:12 KJV).

## GOD'S OWN "TRANS" WORD

God has His own "trans" word, and it comes with serious warnings. The word is *transgression*. To transgress means, "to rebel; to trespass; to break away from truth." The word comes from two Latin words: *trans*, which means *"the other side,"* and *gradi*, which means *"to go over."* In other words, in Latin the word transgress means "to go over to the other side."

From a biblical perspective, to transgress means to know God's laws and commandments but to willfully step over the line of truth and follow sin, disobedience, and iniquity. Committing transgression eventually brings a payday of consequences. The Apostle Paul wrote:

> *"For if the word spoken through angels proved steadfast, and every transgression and disobedience received a just reward, how shall we escape if we neglect so great a salvation..."*
>
> – Hebrews 2:2-3 NKJV

Judas was personally selected by Christ to be one of His twelve disciples, and he was appointed as treasurer of the ministry. Judas had a weakness; he was a thief who pilfered for himself from the money bag (John 12:6). Eventually one silver denarius coin was not enough. When he was offered thirty pieces of silver to betray Christ, he could not resist. We read, *"Judas by transgression fell..."* (Acts 1:25).

You have two paths: one wide and one narrow. You eat from either the tree of life or the tree of knowledge of good and evil. You choose your "trans-train" and take a journey. Transgressions lead to death and destruction, but a spiritual transformation will introduce you to a redemptive covenant. Choose your "trans" wisely.

## THE ULTIMATE GOAL

The world has entered the season of a clash between two kingdoms—the kingdom of God and the kingdom of darkness. In the parable of the wheat and tares, Christ exposed this conflict as a struggle between the children of Satan and the children of God. Satan wants to engage in a tug of war to pull humanity across a line that, when the game ends, leads a person to eternal destruction.

The cultural clashes—the alternative and trans lifestyle, the rejection of traditional marriage and mockery of the marriage covenant, the loss of liberty, and the religious persecution of believers—are the aftermath of unseen spiritual battles, with demonic forces attempting to control the global population. Satan himself offered Christ a political position if He would only take a knee and recognize Satan through the act of worship. Satan showed Jesus all the kingdoms of the world and told Jesus that all this has been delivered to him, and he will give it to whomever he wishes. "If you will worship me, it all will be yours," Satan told Jesus (Luke 4:5-7 ESV).

Perhaps that explains why it is hard to find a nation where the leaders are truly people of faith who believe in the one true God and practice the principles of the Bible. The nations are in the wrong hands—hands that worship the god who still thinks he can promise them the world, if they will only worship him.

This daily assault of faith from all fronts has one intended purpose, which is revealed in Daniel 7:25. In context, the prophecy explains one of the primary plans of the future Antichrist. It reveals the strategy of the *spirit* of antichrist, before *the* Antichrist—the man—is revealed:

> *"And he shall speak words against the Most High, and shall wear out the saints of the Most High; and he shall think to change the times and the law; and they shall be given into his hand until a time and times and half a time."*
>
> – Daniel 7:25 (ASV)

This portion of Daniel was written in Aramaic. "Wear out" is the word *bala*, which refers to "oppressing" or "mentally wearing down" those who are following the Lord and are called saints, which is the original word for one who is set apart and holy. When this spirit is released, part of the wearing down of the righteous involves the changing of times and law. In Aramaic, changing the times and law can refer to changing the actual times (calendar time) and the laws to fit a new system or agenda. The spirit of antichrist is strong enough to influence judges in local, state, and national courts to pass legislation that, in the eyes of God and according to Scripture, are transgressions and abominations.

The moral, political, and cultural clash between light and darkness, truth and lies, honesty and deception, and right and wrong, is intended to mentally wear down a righteous person. Weariness can suppress the joy of the Lord which is your strength (Neh. 8:10). When your strength is missing, your ability to continue standing firm will falter.

## ACCEPTANCE THROUGH REPETITION

In 1939, when the movie *Gone with the Wind* was released, actor Clark Gable's character, Rhett Butler, caused a national stir when he used a four-letter word of profanity. Eighty-four years later, in movies and on television, it is common to hear every profane word. It is also common for God's name to be taken in vain.

Consider what you thought when you first saw two people of the same gender kissing on television. Morally responsible people were shocked and likely expressed their thoughts on the matter. Yet, after seeing this dozens of times, the conscience can become calloused (Paul used the phrase, "seared with a hot iron" in 1 Timothy 4:2). The upcoming generation is always more accepting of new attitudes, ideas, and concepts that the previous generation rejected, simply because they grew up with it.

Once the door was opened, one step at a time, the country arrived at this day. The propaganda machine, most film directors, and all who are under the control of the antichrist spirit understand that moral and biblical principles, which establish the concrete foundation in one generation, can be cracked and even destroyed and rebuilt in the next generation—all through the gradual practice of repetition.

It is the same principle with certain religious groups. The statement, "Give me a child until he is seven, and I will show you the man" is originally attributed to Aristotle. In parts of the Middle East, Muslims as well as Christians send their children to Catholic schools, as they are considered the best place to receive an education. Among the Catholics, most who were raised to attend mass each week will continue to do so as they grow older. This is the principle of planting repetitious seeds in a young mind so that the impact will remain when they become adults. Children are being targeted today because people understand that, if you train them at a young enough age and repeat the training often enough, children will grow up with a lifelong acceptance of whatever they were taught.

We see this same thing happening with our electronic wizardry, and now we see it coming with artificial intelligence. We became convinced that these things would make our lives better and easier and that we needed them for the benefit of humanity. In the beginning, we might have rejected them and thought we could do without them. But gradually, we accepted these things, then woke up one day and realized that what we thought we needed has wasted our time and only made us more dependent on technology. We became the hamster on a wheel, running nowhere fast and wondering how to get the wheel to stop.

## CHAPTER 9

# CRYPTO AND DIGITAL GLOBAL CURRENCY

Experts say that technology grows exponentially, with computer speed and power doubling every eighteen months to two years since the 1960s. We constantly read articles and reports of some new technology that will transform our lives. My grandparents never would have imagined that one day we would have telephones that we carry in our pockets. Their first telephone was a dial-up phone that connected to the wall, with a telephone company operator who would look up phone numbers and tell you the time when you dialed zero. In those days phones had party lines where several neighbors shared the same phone number, so they were on the same line. You knew if the call was for your household because of the number of telephone rings. Since several neighbors were on the same line, this meant that, if your neighbor was talking on their phone, it was possible to pick up your phone and hear their conversation.

The average person living in the mid-20th century wouldn't have imagined the power of the internet, let alone a smartphone that connects to the internet, allows for text messaging, and serves as a camera that shows pictures instantly. When we go to Israel, we used to haul around heavy, bulky studio camera equipment. Last year we recorded on the latest iPhone.

Technology has expanded so much in forty years that the amount of information that once required enough computer equipment to fill a 10,000-square-foot room can now fit in a device that's held in the palm of your hand.

In 2009, new technology was introduced that people said would eventually impact buying and selling. Called Bitcoin, it was the first cryptocurrency ever created. To this day, nobody has verified the identity of the computer programmer(s) who launched Bitcoin, but the pseudonym for the person or persons is Satoshi Nakamoto. Nine years ago, a Japanese American by that name came forward and said he wanted to clear his name. He was not involved with cryptocurrency and had no involvement with Bitcoin. At the time Bitcoin was supposed to have been developed, he was working somewhere else as a government contractor. He thinks perhaps someone used a fictitious name, and it just happened to be his name.

It took a couple of years for the price of one Bitcoin to reach one dollar. In the beginning, the cost for one coin was a fraction of a penny. Bitcoin has had a volatile trading history, but it reached an all-time high of $68,789 per coin in November 2021. It seemed that everywhere we turned, people were investing in cryptocurrency and riding the prosperity wave. At its peak, even teenagers were investing a thousand dollars and getting a return of four thousand dollars. Despite this, Bitcoin was designed to be a payment system, not an investment system.

Bitcoin owners are given a unique private key, or password, to access their wallet. If they lose or forget their password or if the password is stolen, the owner loses access to their coins. Roughly twenty percent of Bitcoins have been forgone because people lost their password and could no longer access their coins.

The success of Bitcoin spawned other cryptocurrencies, but today, Bitcoin still leads the pack. Some cryptocurrencies have been successful, while others have gone out of business, and people lost money.

Sam Bankman-Fried became one of the wealthiest people in crypto after he launched a crypto exchange in 2019 named FTX. Television business analysts were recommending his exchange as a great investment, and in 2022, FTX was valued at forty billion dollars. Bankman-Fried met and was photographed with many politicians, particularly on one side of the aisle. He has a trail of contacts with certain political leaders in Washington who wanted his financial support. Bankman-Fried's personal wealth peaked at $26.5 billion; not bad for a thirty-year-old.

Then in 2022, FTX collapsed and came crashing down. In the aftermath, it was learned that FTX had taken money from Ukraine and moved the money, an estimated forty million dollars in donations, to certain politicians during the 2022 midterm elections. People noted that Congress had funneled billions of dollars to Ukraine, and Ukraine funneled millions to FTX for donations to Congress. It didn't take a tinfoil hat to recognize that this sounded like a conspiracy of money laundering. Some people have said they suspect the amount Bankman-Fried donated to congressional candidates was closer to a billion dollars because a lot of money disappeared, and it had to have gone somewhere. Once FTX collapsed, ordinary customers were unable to withdrawal any funds. The FTX scandal is said to be one of the biggest financial frauds in U.S. history.

Cryptocurrency uses blockchain technology, which is supposed to be safe. But in 2022, Bitcoin owners lost $3.8 billion to hackers. It also didn't take long for scammers to figure out how to use the system to steal other people's money, as people have invested in cryptocurrency companies and lost everything. Before dropping money into cryptocurrency, do plenty of legitimate research and heed the warnings.

For those who are eager to jump on the next shiny new object of technology, Bitcoin and cryptocurrency represented one more exciting breakthrough. For those who are more cautious, especially the older generation, most of us are less trusting of electronic devices, including those with strange voices that answer your questions. Older people don't like the idea of not using cash or of depending on a mobile phone app for financial transactions. We don't like the risk of being hacked and having our bank accounts drained by thieves or of being tracked by nefarious actors. Call us conspiracy theorists, but the older you are, the more opportunities you've had in life to recognize a potential risk when you see one.

The perception of cryptocurrency as a dream come true, along with rapid investments by people who saw a chance to get rich overnight, reminded me of the late 1920s. Enthusiasm for the stock market was high, and untrained people imagined themselves to be stock trading experts. As the saying goes, even the shoeshine boys were giving stock tips. Stock share prices were reaching an all-time high. People who didn't know what they were doing but had been convinced they could get rich overnight, handed their paycheck over to unscrupulous brokers who promised instant prosperity.

On October 28, 1929, known as Black Monday, the stock market dropped and continued to slide through the summer of 1932. Many people lost everything, including jobs. Businesses closed, and the dreams of millions of people disappeared like fog in sunlight. People even committed suicide.

A banking crisis followed, in which people ran to their banks demanding cash for their deposits. In 1932 alone, over fourteen hundred banks collapsed, and depositors lost $725 million in deposits. Eleven thousand banks failed throughout the Great Depression, as the American economy turned apocalyptic.

When Bitcoin and other cryptocurrencies came along, it seemed that the cycle might be repeating itself. In some ways it did, in ways previously mentioned.

The eventual switch to a cashless society, whether cashless means cryptocurrency or central bank digital currency (CBDC), is prophetically inevitable. Once the world began to introduce everything digital, they weren't going to leave fiat currency alone. In 2023, the United States federal government rolled out an instant payment service called Fed Now. The Federal Reserve claims they have made no decision on issuing a central bank digital currency that replaces U.S. fiat currency, but most of the public isn't buying this, especially when we can see the handwriting on the wall.

In March of 2023, four Democrat lawmakers co-sponsored a bill, which was *not* passed by the House chamber, that would order the Treasury Department to take steps to implement a digital currency minted by the government. This was called the eCash Act.

In the spring of 2023, the International Monetary Fund announced the launch of a central bank digital currency (CBDC) called Unicoin, saying this could radically transform the status quo of the global payments and financial system. The IMF does not like the idea of decentralized cryptocurrencies.

Cash is on the way out in many countries, and one day, the United States will follow the rest of the world into the establishment of a cashless society. Once every nation has implemented a digital currency, it's a short jump to banning independent cryptocurrencies and a short jump to one global digital currency.

Why would a government want to control independent cryptocurrencies? For one reason, they want the tax revenue. People who control their own money for buying and selling outside the normal commerce and monetary system might not report the income if they want to avoid paying taxes on the earnings. Even corrupt governments and their leaders can engage in illegal activities using cryptocurrency.

People who participate in illegal activities, such as money laundering, can hide many of their activities if they are primarily using cryptocurrency for their monetary transactions. I have known individuals who, in their past, were illegal drug traffickers who worked with cartels in Columbia and Mexico. The amount of money that passed through their hands was astronomical and almost impossible to imagine. A man told me that he traveled to Columbia and saw a huge warehouse with crates of cash from the floor to the ceiling. Some of it had sat so long it was infested with rats. There was more money than the cartel could launder, and all of it was U.S. currency.

The primary reason for global currency is that governments whose leaders are focused on global power want full control of currency for ordinary citizens. If the currency is controlled, everything the people spend money on can be controlled. With that, the people can be controlled. China already controls who is permitted to participate in society by using a social credit score system that is based on a person's behavior. Citizens who obey the Chinese communist government are allowed to participate in society. Those who disobey the government are not permitted to do certain things, such as travel on public transportation or send their children to school.

China's social credit score system regulates credit, enables government agencies to share data with each other about people, and promotes state-sanctioned moral values. While the media and the Chinese propagandists try to downplay the negative effects of this system, stories that come out of China tell a different tale. Social credit scoring is specifically designed to control behavior through a system of rewards and punishments.

Despite what we are led to believe, the Chinese social credit score is not about determining a person's creditworthiness—that is, their history of paying off bills and loans. This score is based on daily actions. Did you recycle properly? Did you jaywalk? Did you refuse to wear a mask when the government told you to? Did you spread unapproved information on WeChat? Did you criticize government policy? Did you talk about religion? Did you drive your car too fast? Did you win a national sports competition? (Extra points for that.)

A Chinese business with a low social credit score can lose their license, be prohibited from engaging in the trade of goods and services—including imports and exports, be prohibited from trading securities, and a long list of other prohibitions and restrictions. The business is blacklisted until they learn to comply and engage in government sanctioned activities to increase their social credit score.

Even American businesspeople who visit China cannot use cash in many restaurants and stores in the cities. They must download an app on their mobile phone for their purchases. One man who attempted to pay with the Chinese yuan discovered that even China's own yuan currency was not accepted in the shops.

Cameras are also strategically placed throughout the country to watch every move people make, including whom they speak to on the street. The government can recognize people, not just with facial recognition, but from the back, by their gait. In 2014, the Chinese government used new technology to monitor what people said, did, bought, read, and searched on the internet.

In a video for Prager U, a young Chinese man reported that in 2014, the government established a pilot program in forty-three cities across China. Here is how it works. In one city, every person was assigned one thousand credit points. The government added or removed points for individuals, based on how closely their public and private behavior conformed to government standards. For example, buying diapers is fine, but criticizing the government is unacceptable and deducts points. [54] Smoking in a non-smoking area subtracts points. Posting unapproved news stories online causes a loss of points. Lose points, lose privileges.

What kinds of privileges might a citizen lose? Things we take for granted, such as obtaining bank loans, accessing faster internet, traveling by plane or train, buying property, and sending children or grandchildren to school. Muslim Uyghurs receive even more intense scrutiny. They might be sent to a reeducation camp for unacceptable behavior, and their families might never hear from them again.

With the proper number of points, a citizen might get priority health care or deposit-free public housing. They'll be permitted to ride public transportation, and their children might be allowed to attend a university.

This is our modern-day example of a totalitarian regime in action—one that uses surveillance and technology to control their citizens' ability to buy, sell, and live in their own society. One can only imagine the level of technology China has implemented to allow them to minutely track so many people.

The young man reporting for Prager U is concerned that what he sees in China is starting to happen in the West; for example, the government mandating vaccines to keep a job, banks being pressured not to give loans to disfavored businesses, and parents being labeled domestic terrorists for protesting school curriculum. He warns that, if we are not vigilant, it will not end well for us.

Many Western journalists and the proponents of China's value and economic system try to paint a positive picture of the Chinese scoring system. Many of our own political leaders praise China as a model for the United States to emulate. But the fact is, this system *was designed* to examine the behavior of citizens and judge their obedience, and then punish or reward the people accordingly.

One day a global government will demand that same worldwide control of all people and all currency, which will result in the government's ability to control buying and selling, traveling, and participation in all areas of society. If you are not compliant, you will be deemed unacceptable and useless. No government that wants to control the people with an iron fist will ever allow independent thinking; nor will they allow independent cryptocurrencies because they must control the currency to control the people.

The more the citizens of every nation are willing to stand against systems of government control and keep their government leaders—local, state, and national—from implementing tyranny, the longer the nations will remain free. We haven't been able to stop everything the government has foisted upon us. But for the time being, we can still raise our voice and vote the wrong people out of office if we will make the effort to get involved. We know prophetically that one day this system will be implemented globally for a short time, and we know the consequences for anybody who will not comply. Still, there is no reason for us to accept this system prematurely and live under the crush of tyranny.

A well-known political figure gave a speech recently in which he warned of three things related to government overreach:

1. Any power that government takes from the people will never return to them voluntarily.
2. Every power the government takes, it will ultimately abuse to the maximum extent possible.
3. Nobody ever complied their way out of totalitarianism. The only thing we can do is resist.

Unless the citizens rise against the power grab, the only thing that will slow the implementation of government-controlled digital currency and the social credit score system—outside of divine intervention—is a lack of smartphones, along with a widespread and long-term disruption of internet coverage and technology.

At this point, not every person has a smartphone. Some areas have limited internet access and dead zones where there is no cell phone service and no internet. If you had to pay for your food or gas with an app in those areas, you'd be in trouble. Another thing that's needed to operate a cell phone is electricity to keep the phone charged.

Younger people are addicted to their smartphones, while older people generally are not, and some still use an older style phone. Thirty years ago, we used the telephone only when we were home to accept or make the call, or when we found a payphone and had a quarter handy to drop in the payment slot. We had no ability to send text messages and we had no internet. We used snail mail—the postal service. This has changed so much over the last decade that even a toddler will have a meltdown if someone takes away the phone or electronic device. It is nearly impossible for most young people to go half an hour without checking messages or social media. They are addicted at a young age.

Any new and exciting technology that comes along is immediately accepted by a younger generation, without consideration of the long-term consequences of that technology. Once they are presented with the idea of technology that will improve their lives or give them an ability they currently don't have, there is no doubt that many will be at the front of the line to try it.

As of 2020, the global population of people under age twenty was 2.6 billion. Another 2.3 billion were between ages twenty and thirty-nine, for a total of 4.9 billion people aged thirty-nine and under. The age sixty and over population was under 1.1 billion.

Many of those 4.9 billion under the age of forty grew up in the age of new technology. In their lifetime, artificial intelligence and transhumanism will become household words, and these 4.9 billion people will make decisions in the future. The thrill of exploring new technology and discovering new information makes life easier in some ways, but information overload has reset the human brain and created an addiction to technology and gadgets. The question for the future is, will the upcoming generation choose technological advancements that enhance society? Or will they choose technology that destroys it?

# CHAPTER 10

# OLDER CITIZENS IN AN AI WORLD

A few years ago, I received a phone call from the pastor of a large church whose congregation was primarily age forty and under. He expressed concern that they all seemed to be attached to their phones and other electronic devices, to the point of addiction. They used phone apps for banking, buying, selling, and seemingly every aspect of their lives. The pastor's concern was that their love of new technology was preparing them to openly and without reservation accept the beast system. To this group, most of whom were new Christians, it seemed almost ludicrous to warn them not to place a mark in their hand. If they thought it would improve their lives, add convenience, or simply give them a new toy, they would jump on it.

It's strange to observe some of the uses of technology that our current generation has embraced. The idea of becoming a transhuman cyborg through technology is particularly appealing to some. In the book, *To Be a Machine*, the author describes transhumanism as the expression of the human who longs to transcend the confusion and sickness of the body that is cowering in the darkening shadow of its own decay. Technology proponents, most of whom are atheists, note that the problems of life that once were addressed by religion have become the purview of science and technology.

Some use technology to try to defy death, while others use it as an advanced toy. When someone implants a magnetic chip in their finger so they can pick up metal objects, most people over the age of sixty are not impressed. They are asking: "Why? What's the point? What value does this add to your life?"

When people implant chips so they can open doors and turn on lights automatically, the older generation wants to know, why? Why is this necessary? Are we becoming so lazy that we don't want to open a door or turn on the lights by ourselves, so now we need implanted chips to do this for us?

MindWave is another type of unusual technology that converts the energy of the brain so that a person can control external objects using just their own thoughts. The user wears a headset with an electrode placed on the forehead that reads brainwave signals and interprets them. The idea is that the energy generated by the brainwaves will enable the user to accomplish a task with faster learning. They might be able to operate an object, such as a drone, without using a handheld console, or control specially filmed movies with brainwaves.

One of the seven-minute movies available for download gives this description: "…the first in a series of short interactive horror/thriller movies with multiple endings and plot lines that change, depending on your thoughts and emotions. Come face to face with a demon as an acclaimed exorcist and use your mental focus and calm to save three lives...one being yours."

Does that sound like something you'd want your grandchildren experimenting with? We should be alarmed that some of the technology available to the public is making us less intelligent, less creative, less able to interact with humans on a personal level—and more able to interact with demons.

## DO YOU WANT YOUR BRAIN HACKED?

In 2007, an executive from India named Salim Ismail gave a speech at Yahoo company headquarters titled, "The Need to Reengineer the Human Brain." Ismail told attendees that the brain is flawed, and we need to design a better one. He said that our brain is poorly programmed, and technology needs to rewire brains to fix glitches, like stupidity and violence. Another biotechnician spoke on "Mind Uploading: How to Really Do It." This was a proposal for uploading the human brain and consciousness to a computer.

That summarizes the transhumanist's thoughts on a brain. It's just a poorly evolved object in the skull for technocrats to reprogram, redesign, and download.

Yuval Harari says that humans are no longer mysterious souls; we are now hackable animals. Speaking at the World Economic Forum in 2020, Hurari said, "Just imagine North Korea in twenty years where everybody has to wear a biometric bracelet, which constantly monitors your blood pressure, your heart rate, your brain activity, twenty-four hours a day. You listen to a speech on the radio by the great leader, and they know what you actually feel. You can clap your hands and smile, but if you're angry, they know you'll be in the gulag tomorrow morning." [55]

Why would we want to be hacked? This idea of hacking humans, surveilling people, rewiring our "poorly programmed" brains, and creating human cyborgs could be seen as a religion of science and philosophy, practiced by people who claim to have no religion.

Notice how, over the last few years, we have been told to blindly "trust the science." Even when our own brains warn us that the tale we are being told to believe is not science and is not trustworthy, we are still told to shut up and trust the science. Experts who disagree with the unproven claims of pseudoscientists are censored. People repeat the line, "I trust the science," without understanding what they're trusting and without listening to dissenting voices. Are we being conditioned to accept transhumanism through the blind trust of sham science? What else are we being conditioned to accept through blind trust?

Transhumanists make statements such as:

- We want hands on involvement in controlling our genetic makeup.
- We want the right to be around a hundred years from now or a million years from now. A person is free only when there is no death.
- The shift from animal-human to post-human is rapidly accelerating. We are learning to replace organic body parts and organs, so why can we not create back up bodies?
- We are at a turning point. Since evolution isn't working in our favor, we must not submit to the tyranny of nature. We must take matters into our own hands and refuse to die.

It's frightening to think that some people might live forever. Consider Hitler, who had a transhumanist dream of an Aryan race that was obligated to rule the world. Nobody in their right mind would have wanted Hitler to live forever. There are plenty of other tyrants and despots who have ruled throughout the world, and nobody grieved when they died.

There is a great gap between the younger generation and the older generation when it comes to accepting this kind of technology, but there is an even greater gap between the transhumanist religion and the religion of the God of all creation. A generation with no moral compass, no biblical knowledge, no Judeo-Christian beliefs, and no concern for end-time prophecies has no idea how any of this will impact them in the future. They're only looking to create an eternal reign without Christ. They want a utopian world where they can live forever without judgment and without being born again.

## SMALL TOWNS VERSUS THE CITIES

Fads, fashions, and changes in moral ideas and social issues typically begin on the West Coast. We used to have a saying, "As California goes, so goes America." Hollywood and everything branching off that industry has had a profoundly negative effect on the United States and the rest of the world.

The same is true for technology giants in California's Silicon Valley. Technology created there is embraced globally, and an idea that begins with a claim to help humanity can easily become a nightmare. Everything changes once decision making is placed in the hands of greedy people with no biblical and moral foundation.

California has some wonderful churches and plenty of Bible-believing Christians. But much that we see coming from the state has an anti-biblical and far left-leaning slant, which has helped fuel the cultural battles in our country. Government leaders make decisions about the future of citizens and their children, all without input from those affected.

We look at California and see how the leadership's leftist mentality and warped ideas of freedom have failed people. The secular movie and music industries have turned innocent young people into objects of a satanic occult, as the youth have sold their souls for fame and fortune. In the cities of Los Angeles and San Francisco, homeless people are living on streets and in public parks. Trash is piled up, and people in San Francisco say that they must dodge human feces as they walk down the sidewalks. Many people who work cannot afford the exorbitant cost of housing.

Laws have been passed that essentially decriminalize theft if the value of stolen goods doesn't exceed $950. Employees stand back and record with their phone cameras as gangs rush into stores and steal whatever they want, while nobody gets arrested or prosecuted. Anybody who dares defend themselves from a criminal might find the tables turned, as the victim is arrested and the criminal walks free. Environmental laws are passed that make it impossible for some businesses to operate in that state. People who want to flee California cannot find enough moving vans to rent. Long gone are the days when the world wants to emulate the failing state of California—or most cities in the United States, for that matter.

Small town America, on the other hand, has a reputation for being more conservative. We witness this in every presidential election, where we can look at a map and see that a few large cities in the United States vote for the far-left candidate, while the rest of the country votes for the moderate or conservative candidate. Most large cities are run by leftist extremists, and these are the places with uncontrollable crime. These are the cities that experience riots, theft, and the burning down of businesses. Compared to most cities, rural and small-town America are completely different worlds—morally, politically, and spiritually.

It's true that young people often leave small towns for more opportunities in the cities. That leaves an older generation that has lived and thrived on the land. They are people who know their neighbors and know how to care for each other. They can sit on their front porch with family and friends, drink tea, and have a long conversation without a constant ping or ring of a mobile phone. They gather in the mornings at a locally owned restaurant to catch up on the news. They barter, still use cash, and live a simpler and less stressful life. They have survived just fine without a lot of new technology.

If you explained transhumanism and cyborgs to rural America and asked if they'd like to become one, they'd laugh and say, "Do I look like I fell off an apple cart yesterday?" If you showed them your implanted magnetic chip that picks up metal nails, they'd show you their horseshoe magnet from the hardware store and demonstrate how it's more effective than your chipped finger.

People in small towns have nothing to hide, and they're good at hiding nothing. Still, they don't like the idea of technology tracking them. They don't want to be hacked or have their brains rewired. They don't want elitists on either side of the country or somewhere in Europe imposing their will on them, or stealing their land, their cattle, and their way of life.

These are people who believe in God. Even people who don't attend church regularly are open to the Gospel, and they'll freely discuss it with you. They might invite you inside to talk about it over dinner. Even sinners in rural areas recognize when something is unbiblical and bad for the country.

Meanwhile, those who leave small towns and their families for greener pastures in the city are running faster and faster to stay ahead. They're ordering front door-delivered meals on an app, where they'll eat dinner alone and waste time scrolling through their phone or watching a movie. They barely know their neighbors, and it might be safer *not* to know some neighbors. They're convinced the strangers they interact with online are their friends. They generally don't attend church, and anybody who talks about conservative principles or Bible prophecy is considered a tin-foil hat wearer. No wonder they long to become a cyborg.

The best thing a small community can do is keep living the simple life. Have the courage to stand firm for what you believe. Say *no* to political leaders who want to push their unwanted and undesirable agenda on you. Pay attention to the value system of the leaders you vote for. Hold them accountable. Don't be shy about holding to your moral and spiritual beliefs and integrity. The same advice holds true for anybody who wants to live in an environment of freedom and liberty—even if you find yourself stuck in California.

As the older generation, we can't deny that technology has brought some great benefits to humanity. But people with no moral compass and no concept of eternity should not control technology that affects us. When humans try to become God, those with biblical knowledge understand exactly how that experiment is going to end.

## CHAPTER 11

# END-TIME TECHNOLOGY PROPHECIES

The world's three monotheistic religions—Christianity, Islam and Judaism—have a combined estimated total of around four billion adherents. While they have differing theological and ideological beliefs, the three religions have five things in common.

First, each has their holy book. Christians have the Bible, Jews accept the Torah and the Prophets (the biblical Old Testament), and Islam has the Quran and the Hadith. Second, all three believe in the supernatural existence of angels and demons. Third, all have some form of teaching on heaven (or paradise) and the existence of a place of torment for wicked people, known as hell or the underworld. Fourth, there are beliefs among each that their followers will one day stand before God and be judged for the good and evil done in life. Fifth, all three religions have a belief that God spoke through prophets and revealed the future, including signs that would take place at the end of days. Many of these signs would involve strange cosmic activity and destructive natural disasters.

Much of the world follows some form of religion. Many are monotheists (they follow one God), while the rest of the world's religions are polytheistic (they follow many gods). Among the ancient religions, as far back as the Egyptians, Assyrians, Babylonians, Persians and Greeks, adherents of these religions built temples for worship or for people to bring sacrifices to specific gods. Among these ancient religions, there were priests and priestesses, prophets and prophetesses, and magicians along with wise men.

## THE CLASH OF THE GODS

The Hebrew prophet Moses encountered two chief magicians in Egypt named Jannes and Jambres, both supernaturally empowered to turn their wooden staves into living serpents. In the Torah story, a confrontation occurred before Pharaoh involving Aaron and Moses, who represented the Hebrew God, and these two noted Egyptian occultists. Aaron's staff transformed into a serpent and swallowed the rods of the two Egyptians, thus winning phase one of the battle of God versus the gods. Ten plagues and weeks later, the spiritual clash concluded with only one God prevailing against ten false gods of Egypt. This God's name was revealed to Moses as "I Am," or specifically, Yahweh.

The clash continued in a different form in the days of the Babylonian Empire. During this time, the Hebrew God was sending troubling dreams to the Babylonian king named Nebuchadnezzar. He sent for his wise men who were allegedly gifted in reading the cosmic signs and interpreting dreams and strange omens. The wise men failed to provide a clear understanding of these dreams and could not interpret their bizarre symbolism. Only one man, a Hebrew exile named Daniel, had the skills required to interpret symbolism and provide the correct interpretation. Daniel was able to interpret two major dreams for the king and provide the meaning of visions he received, thus revealing histories and empires represented in the symbolism of wild beasts and animals.

Over five hundred years later, another group of wise men set out from the land south of Israel, traveling long distances to worship and present valuable gifts to an infant destined to be the King of Israel. The child's birth was revealed to these men through a strange series of cosmic signs that were seen among the heavenly constellations.

When questioned about how they were informed of this infant's birth, they replied, "We have seen His star in the east" (Matt. 2:2). The prophecy of this star rising in Israel was revealed to an early seer named Balaam and had been recorded for centuries in the Torah (Num. 24:17). Some researchers identify this star as a unique conjunction with the planet Jupiter in the neck of Leo the Lion, which in Judaism connects the cosmic lion symbol with the tribe of Judah. Bethlehem, Christ's birthplace, is located on the parcel of land that was promised to the tribe of Judah.

## WHY THE BIBLE IS DIFFERENT

While secularists, agnostics, and unbelievers classify the Bible as a religious book filled with fables, embellishments, and superstitions, one of the strongest defenses for the sixty-six books in the Bible is prophecy. The Torah was written 3,500 years ago, and Scripture tells us that God gave the words to Moses and told him to write them down (Exodus 17:14; 24:4, 34:27, Numbers 33:2, Deuteronomy 31:24-26). The major and minor prophets in the Old Testament recorded their dreams, visions, and predictions over a period between 800 BC and 400 BC.

Biblical prophecy is not newspaper exegesis, where something happens, and then it is proclaimed a prophecy. The prophets revealed details of future events, some four thousand years before they occurred. They did so with such accuracy that, when their words come to pass, this is seen as undeniable proof of divine inspiration.

## THE PROPHECY OF FLYING

From the time of ancient empires up to the nineteenth century, transportation existed in only a few forms. People walked, rode animals, and crossed the oceans in ships, which facilitated economic trade. The 1800s saw the invention of stagecoaches and steam engine locomotives, then automobiles. The Wright Brothers are credited with flying the first powered airplane in 1903, but that was preceded by other attempts in the 1800s.

Isaac Newton, born in 1643, was a noted physicist and mathematician, but also a brilliant Christian. He was a deep thinker who knew the Bible well and, surprisingly, wrote more about Bible prophecy than science. Newton was intrigued with the meaning of prophetic numbers in Daniel and Revelation. Using only the Scriptures, Newton read these verses in Isaiah and made a prediction:

> *"But they shall fly down upon the shoulder of the Philistines toward the west; together they shall plunder the people of the East" (Isaiah 11:14 NKJV)*

> *"Who are these that fly as a cloud, and as the doves to their windows?" (Isaiah 60:8 KJV)*

Isaiah was predicting that the Jews would return to Israel after their exile. Newton wrote that a time would come when the Jews would return from the nations of the world to Palestine. He predicted they would do so by flying.

The infidel Voltaire mocked Newton's belief that men would one day fly. Newton was correct, and Voltaire was wrong. Neither man lived to see the fulfillment of the prophecy, but the day arrived when airplanes were built and used for transportation.

In 1936 the British government, under a mandate from the League of Nations, built an airport in Tel Aviv. The Israelis captured the facility on July 10, 1948, and in 1974, the name was changed to Ben Gurion Airport. Jews from around the world, including those from former Communist countries, *fly* to one location when they return to Israel.

To make this prediction more specific, Isaiah said the Jews would fly "on the shoulders of the Philistines." The Hebrew word for shoulders is *katheph*, a word that alludes to the upper part of the human that carries the load, and it also speak of the slope of a hill. The territory of the ancient Philistines runs along the Mediterranean coastline of Israel. The Ben Gurion Airport, where planes transport millions of people into and out of Israel, is located in the area that would be considered the shoulders of the Philistines.

## EYES TO SEE EVERYTHING

Another prediction that seemed impossible at the time it was written is recorded in the opening chapter of John's apocalyptic vision:

> *"Behold, He is coming with clouds, and every eye will see Him, even they who pierced Him. And all the tribes of the earth will mourn because of Him. Even so, Amen."*
>
> – Revelation 1:7

Early scholars were puzzled by the possible meaning of this 1,950-year-old prophecy. The context is the return of Messiah to rule His kingdom on the earth, and "every eye shall see Him." It would have been impossible when this was written and during 1,900 years of history for every eye to see Him *at once*.

With the introduction of television, news can be aired and seen at the same time across the nation and even the world. However, it required the viewer to sit in front of the television screen. Present technology merges television with computers and computers with smartphones and small electronic devices. Today, an individual can hold a phone, tap a screen, and access news, videos, and live reports from around the world.

Our own Voice of Evangelism media team uses this kind of technology. I can sit behind a desk and look into a television camera, while on the other side of the world, a large screen is set up on a platform. An interpreter uses a public address system and interprets my message in front of an audience that, at times, has reached tens of thousands of people who are sitting on the ground in an open field.

## BUYING AND SELLING WITH NUMBERS

The most noted prediction that could be fulfilled only in the 21st century is found in Revelation:

> *"He causes all, both small and great, rich and poor, free and slave, to receive a mark on their right hand or on their foreheads, and that no one may buy or sell except one who has the mark or the name of the beast, or the number of his name."*
>
> – Rev. 13:16-17 (NKJV)

Since the second century, early church fathers, Bible scholars, and students of prophecy have pored over this prophecy, dissected the words, and compared verses to unlock the mystery of the mark of the beast. The problem of understanding is evident when reading the commentaries from ministers and scholars:

> *"Despite numerous attempts to identify the mark of the beast with names, computers, monetary systems and the like, its precise nature is unknown, remaining to be disclosed as the end draws near."*
>
> – Merrill Unger

> *"I confess my ignorance as to the number six hundred and sixty-six. I cannot present you with anything satisfactory to myself. We find, answering to the number six hundred sixty-six the words apostasy and tradition: but I cannot say anything positive at this point."*
>
> – JOHN DARBY

> *"Irenaeus has only uncertain guesses to offer, and he thinks the Apocalypist intended the name remain hidden till the Antichrist should come. The language, however, implies that it is discoverable by those who have the requisite wisdom; and the command, let him that hath understanding calculate the number, shows that the author expects some to solve the enigma."*
>
> – ISBON BECKWORTH

> *"It seems to me to be one of those seasons which God has reserved in his own power; only this we know, God has written Mene Tekel upon all his enemies; he has numbered their days, and they shall be finished, but his own kingdom shall endure forever."*
>
> – THE MATTHEW HENRY COMMENTARY

In their days, these men were unfamiliar with computers, credit card numbers, bank routing numbers, phone numbers, Social Security numbers, license plate numbers, pin numbers, and other modern technological advances, all requiring numbers. Today, unless a person uses cash, it is virtually impossible to purchase anything without using a number from a bank card, debit card, check, or a phone app that routes through a number. In the 21st century, you are known as much by a number as you are by your name.

This future system, called the mark of the beast, will be controlled by one man and ten nations united under one system. They will have authority to control an entire economic system of selling and purchasing. The use of numbers is a clear clue that this system will be computer based, and perhaps even AI based.

Those who follow the Antichrist and his beast system will receive a *mark* on their right hand or forehead. This could be something visible, or it could be a small chip implanted under the skin. Some suggest it might be a small tattoo that requires a scanner, computer, or electronic device to read. Chip implants have already been approved for medical purposes, and some people are using them for personal reasons. Yuval Harari says that surveillance will go under the skin. Based on his remark, we can speculate that a chip or something similar is already on the globalists' radar screen for worldwide citizen surveillance.

Whole Foods, which is owned by Amazon, has begun to implement a payment method called Amazon One that requires only a scan of the palm to process the buyer's payment. Buyers will no longer need their wallet or phone to purchase goods. They simply hover their palm over the Amazon One device. The system uses palm recognition for identification, payment, loyalty membership, and entry at the locations. Other businesses are increasingly interested in this system, and airport stores, sports venues, and sports stadiums have deployed the technology.[56]

A man in the Netherlands had a contactless payment chip injected under his skin in 2019. Instead of a bank card or smartphone, he scans his left hand near a contactless card reader, and the payment goes through. A 2021 survey of more than four thousand people across the UK and the European Union showed that fifty-one percent would consider a payment chip implant.

This man has more than just a payment chip; he has thirty-two implants. He considers himself a biohacker—someone who puts pieces of technology into his body to improve his performance. He has chips that open doors and imbedded magnets that pick up metal items.[57]

A gentleman we know in the United Kingdom recently told us that someone came to his home and asked if he would participate in an experiment which entailed keeping a device with him for two weeks to track his movements. He was offered twenty pounds (about $25 US) to participate. If he agreed to have a chip implanted in his hand, he would receive two thousand pounds (about $2,500 US) per month.

We cannot be completely certain if the mark in the hand and forehead will be this kind of technology or something yet to come. It could be a technology that is in the planning stages but has not yet been introduced. We do know that the mark is also connected to a religious system, and those who take the mark will also be worshipping the beast and his system as part of their ability to buy and sell.

## AROUND THE WORLD IN ALL NATIONS

One verse in the Bible that never could have been fulfilled until the advent of modern technological devices and global internet connections is Matthew 24:14, *"And this gospel of the kingdom shall be preached in all the world as a witness unto all nations, and then shall the end come."*

From the time of Christ until now, ministers and oversees missionaries have used whatever methods were available in their time and culture to reach people with the Gospel. Some walked from village to village, some (such as circuit riders) rode horses. Some, like the Apostle Paul, traveled by ship. Ministers such as Billy Graham were able to travel to oversees crusades by airplane. For fifty-eight years, Graham traveled by air and preached to millions of people. Rev. Graham's biography states, "He is known as a pioneer in the use of new technologies to preach the Gospel, from radio and television to films and the internet. Beginning in 1989, a series of Crusades via satellite extended his preaching to live audiences in more than 185 countries and territories."

The World Wide Web and the internet have made it possible to reach nearly all nations with the Gospel, without having to use transportation to travel the world. Global Christian television networks, such as Daystar, TBN, God TV, INSP, and a host of state and regional Christian television networks have carried the voices of hundreds of pastors, teachers, and evangelists into homes and onto computers and smartphones of billions of possible viewers. From radio and television to computers and smartphones, information is available like never before.

Billions of people now have access to technology that allows the Gospel to spread around the globe. We are living in the age when the Matthew 24:14 prophecy, spoken by Christ on the Mount of Olives in Jerusalem, can be fulfilled. Spreading the Gospel to all nations of the world is now possible.

A few years ago, God gave me a word that revival will come through the lens of a camera. At the time I wasn't sure exactly how that would transpire or how it would look. It took about three years to see the fulfillment, but for the last couple of years, I have ministered through something we call, "lens of a camera" because of the word God gave.

In one foreign nation, where it would be challenging to preach in person without persecution or government and religious opposition, the host minister places a large screen on the platform, and people come and sit in an open field where there are lights and speakers. I sit in our television studio in Cleveland, Tennessee and minister live on the screen, preaching through an interpreter. Using this method, we have ministered to hundreds of thousands of people and seen many of them receive Christ—sometimes half or more of the audience—and others be healed of sickness and disease, all without ever leaving home.

All these ancient prophecies about flying, about the universal ability to see the same event at the same time, about the requirement to buy and sell with numbers, and about the Gospel reaching all nations are one hundred percent possible in our time. This is more evidence that we are living in the biblically predicted last days. Technology creates a lot of downsides, but this is one of the positive sides. This shows how knowledge can and is being used for the advancement of God's Kingdom.

Could the negative side of technology be used to bring about an astonishing ancient prophecy, recorded by John in Revelation chapter 13 and known as *the mark and the image of the beast*? We will explore that possibility in the next chapter.

## CHAPTER 12

# IS THE IMAGE OF THE BEAST AI?

Before we delve into the image of the beast, let's review what the Bible teaches about the world's final empire. Two prophets, Daniel and the Apostle John, revealed that at the time of the end, one final empire will unite ten nations under one leader. This coalition will dominate the Middle East and parts of Europe. The leader will be a political-military man who will head a huge army that will create wars and overthrow nations. A new religious system will be established, along with a new economic system of buying and selling that will require a mark or some type of number on the right hand or forehead. This leader will be given authority for a forty-two-month period.

The biblical name for the leader of this united coalition is the Antichrist, and his kingdom is known as the "kingdom of the beast." Revelation 13:14-15 tells us that those who dwell on the earth will be told to make an image to the beast that will be given life and will speak.

When John wrote his revelation, the common language spoken at that time, especially in Asia Minor where many churches were located, was Koine Greek. When John wrote about the image of the beast, he could have selected one of three Greek words to explain the meaning of the word *image*. He could have used the Greek word *characte*r, which means "to cut or to stamp out an image," or the word *charagma,* which alludes to the *act of engraving art.* Instead, John used the Greek word *eikon* ten times, from Revelation 13:14 to Revelation 20:4.

We should note that this image of the beast, identified as the future Antichrist, is not a painting or a picture. The Greek word *eikon,* from where we derive the word *icon*—means "a likeness" or "a figure that resembles someone." In Catholic churches, for example, an icon can include an actual statue of Jesus, the disciples, Mary, or a saint.

While there have been counterfeit miracles performed in the name of different religions, the future image of this beast, an image that will speak and have life, has a satanic element connected with it. This will not be a forged miracle using human trickery or sleight of hand illusions. The Bible calls this the work of Satan: "*...whose coming is after the working of Satan with all power and signs and lying wonders*" (2 Thess. 2:9 KJV). Jesus warned that "*false Christs and false prophets will rise and show great signs and wonders to deceive, if possible, even the elect*" (Matt 24:24 NKJV).

## LEGEND OF THE GOLEM

A few students of prophecy have suggested that the image of the Antichrist may be linked to a well-known Jewish legend about the creation of a golem. The Hebrew word golem means "shapeless mass." The golem was a creature made from the earth and shaped like a human being, which was created for the purpose of serving its creator. According to the best-known version of the story, Jewish Rabbi Judah Loew ben Bezalel brought to life a golem that he formed from clay. The golem's task was to deal with those, namely some Christians, who were persecuting the Jews living in the city of Prague.

Jewish enemies had falsely accused the Jews of mixing the blood of Christian children in their flour and water when making the Jewish matzo bread. This lie, known as blood libel, incited violent retaliation against Jews living throughout Prague.

The chief rabbi of Prague realized that danger was coming. One night he dreamt of the city on fire and lying in ruins. In the smoke and ashes, the word *golem* was written. The rabbi knew that a golem was a creature made of clay that was mentioned among the writings of some Jewish mystics. The creature, according to the tradition, could be created only by a tzaddik, or a righteous man.

As the legend continues, the rabbi took his son-in-law and his top student to the clay banks of the Vltava River. At midnight, he prayed and formed a creature like a man. Using mystical words and the sacred name of God (YHVH), the creature began to move. The rabbi wrote the word *emet,* which means "truth" on the forehead of the creature, then commanded the golem to awake.

According to the legend, the rabbi instructed the golem to protect the Jews and capture their enemies. It worked for a while, but the golem eventually became a threat to even the Jewish community. The golem had to be stopped, which the rabbi accomplished by erasing the letter alef in the word emet, leaving the word *met,* which in Hebrew means "death." Thus, the golem came to his end.

Another legend says that the golem would come to life when God's name was written on parchment and placed in the golem's mouth or on his arm. To stop the creature, God's name was removed from the golem.

This legend caused a few people to speculate that the future false prophet could be from a Jewish background and be familiar with the legend of the golem. They think that since the golem allegedly came to life after the three Hebrew letters, *alef, mem* and *tav* were written on the *forehead,* this could be linked to the mark of the beast, a mark that is made in the right hand or in the forehead (Revelation 13:17-18).

The golem had no soul or spirit, yet it was given "life." The image of the beast *will not*, at least in my opinion, be connected to the golem legend. The similarity to the golem story is that a man will be given life and the ability to speak, through the power and authority of a man called the false prophet (see Revelation 16:13; 19:20; 20:10).

## WHEN A LIFELESS IMAGE SPEAKS AND LIVES

When the Apostle John peered thousands of years into the future and saw the apocalypse, he was shown a startling vision of future economic control by one man under a new and unusual system. I am sure he was uncertain what it meant and how it would be possible. Even biblical scholars who lived from the 1700s to early 1900s noted that *they* were uncertain how this would or could occur. Even a hundred years ago, before the invention of personal computers, electronic tracking devices, and electronic buying and selling, biblical scholars had no idea how such a system could possibly be implemented.

This mystery is recorded in the thirteenth chapter of the book of Revelation with the rise of two men. One is a political leader who is joined by another, a religious leader identified as a false prophet. The second personality arrives with the symbolism of "two horns like a lamb."

> *"Then I saw another beast coming up out of the earth, and he had two horns like a lamb and spoke like a dragon. And he exercises all the authority of the first beast in his presence, and causes the earth and those who dwell in it to worship the first beast, whose deadly wound was healed."*
>
> – Revelation 13:11-12 (NKJV)

In apocalyptic symbolism, a lamb represents Jesus Christ twenty-six times in the New Testament. However, in this scene, the person is not Christ, but comes as a false representative of Christ. In Scripture, horns are symbols of power or authority. The interpretation is that this false prophet will form a new religion by uniting all religions under him. He will particularly focus on the apostate form of Christianity—that is, a claim of Christianity without the real Christ, and one that ignores the sin nature of humanity. The other religion he will try to bring under his control, the second horn, is suggested to be Islam, which is the largest religious group after Christianity.

Judaism, Christianity, and Islam all claim Jerusalem as a holy place, and both are strongly represented in modern Israel and various nations throughout Europe and the Middle East. This area will be the center of this new kingdom and religion. The vision continues:

> *"He performs great signs, so that he even makes fire come down from heaven on the earth in the sight of men. And he deceives those who dwell on the earth—by those signs which he was granted to do in the sight of the beast, telling those who dwell on the earth to make an image to the beast who was wounded by the sword and lived."*
>
> – Revelation 13:13-14 (NKJV)

One reason this new religion will gain credibility in the eyes of global followers is because of the extraordinary miracles that will be performed in the sight of men. Forty years before John received this vision, the Apostle Paul warned of the arrival of the political man (identified as the Antichrist) and said he would be manipulated by Satan to produce "signs and lying wonders" (2 Thess. 2:9). Christ foretold the arrival of this satanic duo, the Antichrist and false prophet, when He warned, *"For there shall arise false Christs, and false prophets, and shall shew great signs and wonders; insomuch that, if it were possible, they shall deceive the very elect"* (Matt. 24:24 KJV).

Just what this fire from heaven might be in Revelation 13:13 is unknown, although this miracle occurred several times in the Old Testament. It happened when the prophet Elijah prayed fire from heaven onto an altar to convince Israel that Yahweh was the true God (1 Kings 18:38). This same prophet called fire from heaven onto fifty soldiers and their captain (2 Kings 1:10). God sent fire on the altar that David constructed on Mount Moriah (1 Chron. 21:26), and when King Solomon built the new temple in Jerusalem, fire descended on the sacrifices (2 Chron. 7:1).

The only time that Satan directed a "fire from heaven" was when Job's animals were consumed by fire, which may have been a storm that caused lightning to strike his livestock (Job 1:16). The false prophet will demonstrate his authority using signs and wonders, including his god-like feat of creating an image that all men will be commanded to worship or else be killed:

> *"And he had power to give life unto the image of the beast, that the image of the beast should both speak, and cause that as many as would not worship the image of the beast should be killed."*
>
> – REVELATION 13:15 (KJV)

Recall that the word image in Greek is *eikon*, meaning "likeness" or "of a similar representation." In this case, the image is a likeness or similar representation of the beast, a word used to describe the man who has reorganized the ancient Grecian, Babylonian, and Persian empires under one coalition.

Looking again at verse 15, the Greek word for power is *didomi,* which simply means that he will have the ability to make the image "live." The Greek word for life is *pneuma*, a word translated as "wind" or "breath," all of which implies that this image will have the ability to think and reason. The image will do something that had previously been unheard of. Something will cause this image to come to life and speak, and the world will become enamored with both the image and the man who had the power to bring the image to life.

## RELIGION LED BY ARTIFICIAL INTELLIGENCE?

A new religious leader is in charge, and Revelation 13:14 says that he will tell all who dwell on the earth "*that they should make an image to the beast, which had the wound by a sword, and did live.*" It appears that every person on the earth will be ordered to make an image (a likeness or similar representation) of the beast, who is the Antichrist.

Some who encourage and promote the use of artificial intelligence have suggested that AI can create a new religion—the possibility of a new AI god. This god would have unlimited knowledge and the skills to answer your most complicated questions. This god would be able to communicate in any human language and have a global following.

Recall that Yuval Noah Harari suggested that artificial intelligence will be able to compose its own religious texts, which will gain a cult following. He suggested that these cult adherents would then be instructed by the computers to kill people. As egregious as most of Harari's statements can be, it is possible he's veered into an explanation for how so many people will die by beheading during the Antichrist's tyrannical rule.[58]

In Europe, many of the mainline denomination churches are becoming empty, as their members grew older and passed away, and nobody reached the younger generation. There is also a shortage of pastors. One evangelical leader said that Europe is one of the toughest areas in the world to witness for Christ because of their secularism, pluralism, and materialism. Much of Europe is skeptical that God even exists.

With the current spiritual condition of much of Europe, and even the Western nations, it seems there are so few people who would stand against anything the beast system pushes, or even understand the implications of biblical prophecy regarding the beast system. People need a wakeup call.

This year, at a church in the Bavarian town of Furth, Germany, three hundred people showed up for forty minutes of prayer, music, and an experimental sermon, all of which was generated by chatbot artificial intelligence. It was presented by a female avatar—a realistic-looking robotic female who was shown on the large screen.

The 29-year-old theologian and philosopher behind the idea, Jonas Simmerlein from the University of Vienna, said that ninety-eight percent of the content comes from the AI machine. He insists this is the way of the future, and we are going to see an effort for humans to stay out of the church service.

Parishioners lined up an hour early to listen to this experimental AI avatar. Some who were interviewed after the service said it was interesting, but the avatar had no personality, or the message was boring, or it wasn't personal enough.[59]

Some large churches conduct a service with music and preaching from one location, then show the service on a screen in other locations. This has been an effective way to reach much of the present generation, as they are accustomed to watching things and gathering information on screens. Could AI generated music and sermons with robotic avatars become the worship leaders and ministers of the future? Will they become more popular than a human operating under the Holy Spirit anointing? Let's hope not. But time will tell.

## THE MEANING OF *AVATAR*

The definition of the word avatar is interesting. *Avatar* is derived from a Sanskrit word meaning "descent." In 18$^{th}$ century English, it referred to the descent of a deity to the earth—typically, the incarnation in earthly form of Vishnu or another Hindu deity. It later came to refer to any incarnation in human form, and then to any embodiment (such as that of a concept or philosophy), whether or not in the form of a person.

In the age of technology, avatar is a word being used to describe the image that a person chooses as his or her "embodiment" in an electronic medium.[60]

People can create their own personal avatars using computer application technology. The result is a cartoon-like character that bears a resemblance to the creator's own features.

A conservative media personality told of going to an Abba concert in 2023 and watching the group perform. Abba is a musical band from the 1970s, and this concert was the band performing, not as humans, but as avatars. The performers looked so real that a family member was shocked to learn the people on stage were not humans.

Will the image of the Antichrist be an avatar? Is this the kind of image people will be forced to create and worship—an avatar? We can't say for certain, but we could be moving in that or a similar direction.

## THE FUTURE ECONOMIC SYSTEM

We are familiar with the conclusion of this narrative, as revealed by John in Revelation:

> *"He causes all, both small and great, rich and poor, free and slave, to receive a mark on their right hand or on their foreheads, and that no one may buy or sell except one who has the mark or the name of the beast, or the number of his name."*
>
> – Revelation 13:16-17 (NKJV)

The combination of a ten-nation political coalition under the control of one man (the Antichrist) coupled with the formation of a new religious system that has never existed before, will allow these two men to create a new system of economic control. The level of control will be significant, because prior to the formation of this new cashless economy, there will have been numerous wars, severe food shortages, plagues, earthquakes, and volcanic eruptions. Many people will have died. Food and water supplies in some areas will be diminished by two-thirds, and in other areas by a third. People will be looking for anybody who comes along as a savior and promises to fix the world's problems.

The process of aligning with this new political-religious system will be through something identified as "the mark of the beast." The power to buy and sell will be given only to individuals who have completely embraced the system and turned to the new world religion. These people willingly reject any other form of religion and serve the Antichrist, embracing the deception and believing that this will enable them to survive the treacherous times.

The economic system will allow a person to engage in commerce using the method identified in Scripture. There will be a mark on the right hand or the forehead—perhaps a chip, a readable tattoo, or something not yet introduced. Numbers are involved. The third identifier on the list is the "name of the beast," which is calculated in an ancient word-numerical system to total six hundred, sixty, and six.

It is clear from Scripture that this system will impact all nations and ethnic groups—the small (ordinary citizens) and the great (leaders), the rich and the poor, the free and the enslaved. This system will cause (that is, force) all to accept and receive this mark.

Those who bear the mark of this system have taken a mark of doom, which is perhaps the most perplexing part of this prophecy. There will be two groups during this time. One group will gladly join the system, perhaps for economic and physical survival. They will follow the Antichrist, take the mark, name, and number of the beast, and become part of the beast kingdom.

The other group will obey the biblical warnings and refuse to join the kingdom of the beast. These people will not take the mark. As a result, the followers of the beast will capture these individuals and execute them in a primitive manner, through beheading (which is a method of execution in many Islamic countries).

All of mankind will receive a warning not to take the mark. They will be warned about the punishments if they do:

> *"Then a third angel followed them, saying with a loud voice, 'If anyone worships the beast and his image, and receives his mark on his forehead or on his hand, he himself shall also drink of the wine of the wrath of God, which is poured out full strength into the cup of His indignation. He shall be tormented with fire and brimstone in the presence of the holy angels and in the presence of the Lamb. And the smoke of their torment ascends forever and ever; and they have no rest day or night, who worship the beast and his image, and whoever receives the mark of his name.'"*
>
> – Revelation 14:9-11 (NKJV)

The doom is not just the torment; it is the eternal separation from God for those who chose to follow and worship the Antichrist and his system.

## THE BIG WHY?

I have been asked the question, "If people are simply trying to physically survive by purchasing food through this system, why would God not give them grace and allow them to feed themselves and their families by using this mark?" The answer is that this entire system is based upon a false religion and the idolatrous act of worshipping the Antichrist and his man-made image.

Consider this example. When the Israelites departed from Egypt, there were six hundred thousand men, not counting the women and children. They departed with unleavened bread but entered a rugged wilderness where they lacked the foods they were accustomed to in Egypt. There was also a shortage of fresh water. Moses left for forty days on Mount Sinai, and the people demanded that Aaron collect their gold earrings and create a golden calf they could worship.

They had lived for hundreds of years among the idolatrous Egyptians, a culture that worshipped a different deity for just about every situation. They also deified and worshipped some mortals; namely, certain rulers. After all that time, the culture had influenced some of these former Hebrew slaves. Several of the Egyptians gods were represented by a cow or a bull, and they all were given names. Each named cow was associated with a particular role, and each had its main center of cult worship. Apis was worshipped in Memphis, Hathor was worshipped in Dendera, and so on.

With Hathor being a cow god that was worshipped in Dendera, a location near the Red Sea where the Hebrews might have crossed, it might be reasonable to assume that the Hebrews could have been creating a golden image to represent this Egyptian god. This god was also associated with music and dance, among other things. By molding a golden calf and dancing around it, the Israelites were turning from trust in their God, Yahweh, who delivered them from slavery with astonishing and supernatural signs and wonders. Instead of turning to God for sustenance and provision, their hearts turned to idol worship, which was an abomination to God. The divine punishment for this act was the death of three thousand Israelites and the destruction of the golden calf.

The true danger of the beast and his image is that the entire system is designed to appeal to those with religious inclinations, but the worship points humanity away from the one true God and toward an image formed by mere men.

## SUMMARY OF THE IMAGE OF THE BEAST

The image of the beast will involve a supernatural satanic miracle that deceives the world. A man called the "false prophet" (Rev. 16:13) will initiate the creation and worship of this image. Christ warned of false prophets arising at the time of the end, showing "signs and wonders" that are so convincing, even the elect could fall for the deceptive miracles (Mark 13:22).

In 1 Kings 18, Baal's false prophets built an altar where they offered sacrifices and cried aloud for hours, asking Baal to send fire on the altar. There was no response, as all idols have stone ears that cannot hear and closed mouths that cannot speak. During six thousand years of history, not once did an image made by men either move, speak, or come alive, although many were worshipped. This satanic miracle will be the first time that a soulless, manmade object of worship manifested life.

It is possible that the image, which is an exact replica of the man called the Antichrist, is some form of man-created image that will be linked to a robot or another form of artificial intelligence. This will allow the image to speak, answer questions, and manifest some form of life. We can imagine that the image could be an avatar or something similar.

Most prophetic teachers agree that the tribulation is seven years in length. This image is created in the middle of the seven years, which is three-and-one-half years into the tribulation. With technology multiplying so rapidly, we can only imagine the level of technology that will be available when the Antichrist arrives on the scene.

When we consider the tribulation judgments on the earth and the subsequent danger to the electrical grids and other manmade systems, perhaps this is why the Antichrist will demand a mark on a person's right hand or forehead. If computer systems fail, an outward visible mark would be one way to identify those who are aligned with the beast system and the false prophet's religion.

## CHAPTER 13

# WILL MYSTERY BABYLON BE A SMART CITY?

Chapters 17 and 18 in the book of Revelation have been a source of theological debate for centuries. John appears to be describing a religious system in chapter 17 and a city with global economic impact in chapter 18. The entire imagery in both chapters is filled with apocalyptic symbolism.

The narrative opens with a woman identified as a great harlot. She is clothed in purple and scarlet and adorned in gold, precious stones, and pearls. She is sitting on a scarlet beast with seven heads and ten horns, and she is holding a golden cup full of abominations.

The imagery is reminiscent of a figure in Greek mythology named Europa, who was known in John's day as one of the women whom Zeus was said to have fallen in love with. When John released his vision, the first interpretation by his readers likely would have been that the woman on the beast represented Europa.

According to mythology, Europa was a mortal, born to King Agenor of Tyre. As she grew to become an adult, Zeus couldn't resist her beauty, so he morphed himself into a white bull and showed up in a field next to the Mediterranean Sea where Europa was picking flowers. She and her attendants were so taken by this lovely tame white bull that

Europa finally climbed onto the back of the bull. Before she could jump off, Zeus carried her into deep waters and across the Mediterranean to the coast of Crete. She gave birth to three sons who were the offspring of Zeus, so the story goes. One of the competing theories for how the continent of Europe got its name comes from this mythological story of Europa and Zeus.

An image of Europa riding a bull can be found on coins and on statues in Europe. One statue is placed in Brussels, Belgium outside the Council of the European Union. Does it seem odd that the European Union would choose the symbol of a married mythological god kidnapping a mortal, whom he then impregnated three times?

Revelation 17:18 reads, *"And the woman whom you saw is that great city which reigns over the kings of the earth."* In John's day, that city would have been Rome, because the Imperial Roman Empire lasted from around 27 BC to AD 476. When John had the vision of events in Revelation, it was believed to be around the year AD 95, so the Romans would have been ruling. Specifically, the emperor Domitian ruled from AD 81–96, while John was imprisoned on the island of Patmos.

Like Nero before him, who had both Peter and Paul beheaded, Domitian was a cruel man who killed his own brother and persecuted Christians. *Foxe's Book of Martyrs* tells us that Domitian issued an order "that no Christian, once brought before the tribunal, should be exempted from punishment without renouncing his religion." Any Christian who swore an oath of allegiance to him would be set free; those who refused were killed. People were bribed to testify against Christians, and many were slaughtered for money. Christians were blamed for every natural disaster that befell the Roman empire. During this time, Timothy rebuked Ephesian pagans for their idolatry, and they beat him so badly with clubs that he died two days later.[61]

John used the terminology "mystery, Babylon the great." Scholars think that one reason John used that term was because the destruction of the Jewish temple in Jerusalem in AD 70 by the Romans and the scattering of the Jews was reminiscent of the same actions carried out by the ancient Babylonians.

In modern times, some have interpreted the woman on the beast to be an allusion to New York City as mystery Babylon. They even suggest that the Statue of Liberty is a symbol that aligns with the woman on the beast. They say this because New York City has been a global center of world trade and finance for decades, although this is rapidly changing. Added to that, some Western Christians believe that New York City is mystery Babylon because they think God is going to destroy the city for iniquity, just as He allowed with Sodom and Gomorrah.

The spirits of lust, greed, and power are found in many places, not just New York City. This three-pronged spiritual stronghold is found in cities and empires throughout history and around the world today. Many cities, including New York City, have parallels to ancient Babylon. But I do not believe the apocalyptic references allude to that city.

## THE WILDERNESS VERSE

Rome is yet another place whose founding involves mythology. The story goes that Romulus and Remus were twin brothers who were conceived when the Roman god Mars impregnated their mother, who was a vestal virgin and the daughter of a former king. The twins were abandoned along the Tiber River to die, but they were saved by another god, claimed to be the father of the river. The boys were suckled by a she-wolf, which is also memorialized with statues in Europe. Years later Romulus and Remus became leaders, but Remus was killed in a dispute with his brother. Romulus went on to establish the city of Rome, which is built on seven hills.

Farming was a popular profession in Ancient Rome because of its soil, long growing season, and temperate weather. The land in Rome and its surrounding areas does not fit the description in Revelation 17:3 where John said, "So he carried me away in the Spirit into the wilderness." That is where John saw the woman sitting on the beast.

The Greek word used for wilderness in that verse is *eremos*, which is "a wasteland;" "an empty, uninhabited place;" "a forsaken, desolate place." The idea is that, when John was shown the vision, the city had been built in a desolate wilderness, yet it was successful in trade. It was alongside a set of rivers where ships traveled for transporting goods. It was called "that great city which reigns over the kings of the earth" (Rev. 17:18).

In Revelation 18, the mystery city of Babylon falls and is destroyed by the ten kings who are in a coalition with the Antichrist. The city of great wealth and world trade will be destroyed in one hour (Rev. 18:17). Those who made a living in the shipping industry stood at a distance, crying and mourning over the city, as they watched it go up in smoke. This city had made them wealthy. Revelation 18:24 also tells us, *"And in her was found the blood of prophets and saints, and of all who were slain on the earth."*

## A FUTURE AI SMART CITY

A city is being constructed right now that could fit this description. When I first saw a report about the plans for this region, I was immediately drawn to the *possibility* that this city could fit many of the descriptions found in Revelation 17 and 18.

One of the world's noted wilderness regions is Arabia, a desert of rock, sand, and mountains mentioned numerous times in the Old Testament. First Kings 10:15 says that, in Solomon's time, the kings of Arabia traded in spices through merchants. The kings of Arabia also brought gold and silver to King Solomon (2 Chronicles 9:14). Jeremiah noted that all the kings of Arabia and all the kings of the mixed multitude dwell in the desert (Jer. 25:24).

In Isaiah 21:1, the prophet writes of the "burden of the desert of the sea." He uses the phrase, *"Babylon is fallen, is fallen"* in Isaiah 21:9, which is the same phrase used by John in Revelation 18:2, *"Babylon the great is fallen, is fallen."* Isaiah 21:13 mentions Arabia and trouble that would be coming.

Saudi Arabia has been known as a leading supplier of oil, helping to bring trillions of dollars into the Middle East for the kings of the nations. Even if Saudia Arabia doesn't run out of oil, they know that there is intense global pressure for other forms of energy to replace oil. The current Crown Prince of Saudi Arabia wants to modernize their country and establish tourism, which will be a dramatic shift for a country that has been perceived for its ancient traditions that set them back from the modern world. One way they are becoming involved in tourism is by opening the traditional site of Mount Sinai, which is located in Arabia, according to Galatians 4:25.

One of the plans of Crown Prince Mohammed bin Salman is to spend an estimated five hundred billion dollars to build the largest and most significant Fourth Industrial Revolution smart city on the planet. The 10,200 square mile city will be called Neom—with neo meaning "new" and M being the first letter of mustaqbal, an Arabic word meaning "future." The city is named Neom to imply "New Future."

A smart city is defined as one that uses artificial intelligence, electronics, and modern technology to monitor and collect data on everything. Resources—that is, land, water, transportation, and so on—will be managed and controlled. Everything and everybody will abide by rules of the green agenda. Make no mistake, in any smart city, citizens will also be monitored, managed, and controlled.

The 10,200 square-mile futuristic region of Neom is being developed in Northwest Saudia Arabia, at the north end of the Red Sea and east of Egypt's Sinai Peninsula, across the Gulf of Aqaba. This location gives easy access to the Suez Canal, a sea-level waterway in Egypt that is a popular shipping route.

The project experienced construction delays, but Neom is currently expected to open in 2039, with certain tourist areas opening in 2026. The plan is highly ambitious, but there seems to be international desire to build and invest in this project.

Neom is preparing to be a model for the rest of the world—an environmentally conscious green city that is a dream come true for globalists, entrepreneurs, technology creators, and climate change billionaires. Cutting edge technology will focus on artificial intelligence, with an airport, high-speed trains (subways), and drones, all powered by renewable energy. It doesn't appear there will be any cars.

An online video advertisement and the website for the project tell us this about Neom:

- It will be a hub for innovation and an entirely new model for sustainable living, with standards never before witnessed.
- Sustainable construction and digital design will merge in a Fourth Industrial Revolution to produce standards by which the global industry will measure itself. Neom represents a transformational movement that will create a new ecosystem to help build smarter, more ethical, and highly profitable industries.
- It will be powered by clean energy.
- Forty percent of the world can be reached within six hours.
- Within Neom are fourteen sectors, spearheaded by the world's best talent: energy; water; mobility; technology

and digital; food; manufacturing; media; entertainment and culture; tourism; sports; design and construction; financial services; health, well-being and biotech; and education. Each sector has been designed to advance technology and push the very limits of human knowledge.

- The entire region will offer unparalleled access to nature. Ninety-five percent of land will be rewilded and preserved.

- A city named Oxagon will be located on the Red Sea, at the crossroads of the world, where thirteen percent of the world's trade occurs via the Suez Canal. The city will have a next-generation port with a fully integrated supply chain system offering easy access and connectivity to global trade routes. Oxagon is dedicated to driving business innovation. It will be powered by 100% renewable energy.

- Trojena will be a year-round mountain destination, ideally located for alpine and adventure sports. The climate is cooler than the rest of the region, and winter temperatures can reach sub-zero. Plans include a 3,000-seat mountainside amphitheater, 36km of ski slopes, hotels, serviced apartments, and retail and dining spaces. This is set for completion by 2026.

- If mountains and snow are not your thing, there is always one of Neom's beautiful islands, perfect for some rest and recreation. Sindalah will be an exclusive island destination in the Red Sea, where luxury is a tribute to nature and a new world is unveiled. The global yachting community is welcome, as well as visitors looking for exquisite luxury. This will be open to the public first.

Finally, we are told that the world needs Neom because the world needs change. "Neom will change how the world does business by making the region a special economic zone, easing the way for entrepreneurs to blaze their trail. It will change the way we live our lives, with competitive health care and the highest standards of livability. And it will change how we look after nature and our planet. Imagine Neom as a prototype for a better future, a future for all. One being built to last. So, when the world asks, 'What is Neom?' you'll know to answer that 'Neom is a place that will change the way we live on this planet. It's simple, really.'"[62]

That's not all. Within Neom are plans for a residential and retail complex called The Line. It will be a 500-meter high, 200-meter wide, 170-kilometer-long enclosed region that will be built in the shape of a straight line. It will have everything its nine-million residents need, all within a five-minute walk, with no cars, no roads, and no carbon emissions.

The Line is advertised to offer a sustainable pattern for a livable future—a new wonder for the world. According to planners:

> *"The Line shows us a new way of doing things. A place that cares for its society. Many demographers think the cities of the future will contain about fifty million people. At The Line, we are creating a template for cities of the future. That's where jobs and opportunities are. Other cities can then compare their plans to what's being done in Saudi Arabia."*

The Line will span three geographical regions—the coastal desert along the Red Sea, the mountains, and the upper valley. The Line will begin at the Red Sea. Designers describe the vision:

> *"It starts out at 500-meters high, and as the topography rises, it disappears into the mountains. There is a hidden marina, created with a canal brought in from the Red Sea. Energy will be produced through solar, wind, and hydrogen. The water is 100% sustainable, using desalinated water from the sea and reusing the salt brine."*

The prototype of the inside design of The Line resembles stacked modules, reminiscent of an elaborate Lego creation. Everything residents need is either up, down, or across from the pod where they will be living. The outside of the long, straight complex is a mirrored glass façade that will reflect the surrounding landscape.[63]

Designers claim the city will provide equality—equal healthcare to all residents who live in The Line, and equal access to education, including higher education. The views inside will be almost surreal in nature, they say. Traveling the hundred miles from one end of The Line to the other will take twenty minutes by train (subway).

Neom, the advertisements say, will bring new technology, new industry, and new services into the Saudi kingdom. Physicist and Professor Michio Kaku visited the project and spoke with three people deeply involved in the design and construction. Kaku is sold on the project, saying, "This is something that will affect the destiny of civilization itself. It's a new way of thinking, of organizing ourselves, and of living. Neom creates the future of the human race."

Neom is not without controversy. First, Saudi Arabia has had a dismal human rights record, and they are building Neom in an area that was the historic home to the Huwaitat tribe. Around twenty-thousand tribe members are being relocated to make room for development. Any member of the tribe who draws attention to the human rights violations or complains about being relocated has either been killed or sentenced to death.

The second issue is the environmental impact. In particular, The Line has been criticized for the 1.8 billion tons of embodied carbon dioxide that the building project is expected to produce. Claims of livability are questioned because that all depends on how the city is maintained and the level of control Saudi Arabia will have over the city.

Like everything else the globalists desire to accomplish, none of those issues will matter. With some people, the end always justifies the means.

## COULD NEOM BE THE ECONOMIC BABYLON?

The first hint that this city could be the one John saw is that "the kings of the earth have been made rich through her." During the Old Testament era, the Hebrews selected a king to rule, the first being Saul, thereby becoming a monarchy. Their second king was David, and the third was Solomon.

In John's day, Roman leaders were called emperors, and the men appointed to oversee lands and cities under Roman occupation were governors and kings. We know of the king named Herod (Matt. 2:1). Four ruled in succession from the time of Matthew 1:1 to Acts 26:27, where we find the mention of a king named Agrippa.

The Middle East is one region of the world where a monarchy rules the Gulf States and several Arab nations. Currently, for example, Jordan's ruler is King Abdullah II. The king of Saudi Arabia is Salman bin Abdulaziz. Other Middle Eastern countries have monarchies, but their rulers currently have the titles Emir, Sultan, or Sheikh.

Revelation 18:3, which speaks of merchants becoming rich through the abundance of her wealth is often compared to early Rome and the trade ships and agreements. However, now we see how that oil from the desert in the Middle East, which has been sold around the world, has brought the oil producing nations trillions of dollars. The plans for

Neom reveal that industry, technology, and every other possible sector will be represented in this region of great wealth. Notice in Revelation that it is the seamen and traders with ships who are grieving the loss of the city.

Once Neom is built, the luxury of the region, along with the technological, environmental, and vacation wonderland it creates, will draw the richest of the world's elites. This won't be a place for ordinary tourists.

Neom's 10,200-square-mile area is the size of Albania. If the entire region, or one or more of the cities within Neom is indeed the mystery Babylon that John saw, the obvious reason for students of prophecy to misidentify it all these years is because it did not yet exist. Indeed, it has been a mystery.

## IS CHINA THE GREAT RED DRAGON?

Another mystery found in Scripture is the red dragon.

Unless things change, the nation of China seems positioned to become a leader of the new world empire. Their government is fascinated with technology, even when they must steal it from other countries. They are becoming the world headquarters for artificial intelligence surveillance technology.

China's *eternal disadvantage* is atheism, the denial of God that will send many people in the nation to hell. Atheism is also their *temporary advantage* because, without belief in the existence of an eternal Creator, every atheist can build their own god—a robotic god, a technological god, or a deity created from artificial intelligence. With no righteous foundation, atheistic leaders don't care about the outcome for citizens. The objective is control at all costs.

Apocalyptic biblical literature is noted for its strange symbolism, but Zechariah, Daniel, Ezekiel, and Revelation often interpret the meaning of the prophetic symbolism. In Daniel, the lion with two wings is Babylon from King Nebuchadnezzar's time. The large bear with three ribs represents the Media-Persia Empire and the three nations they seized when their empires came to power. When the Persian rule ended, the next animal Daniel described was a fast-moving leopard with four wings. History confirms that this leopard was the imagery of Alexander the Great, who formed the Grecian Empire and overtook Babylon.

These same animal images are seen seven-hundred-years later, in Revelation 13, when John described the kingdom of the Antichrist. His kingdom will consume the same three territories, comprised of Egypt, Libya, Ethiopia, Israel, Lebanon, Syria, Iraq, Iran, Afghanistan, Turkey, Greece, Macedonia, and all nations that were part of the three previous empires alluded to in the time from Daniel to Christ.

Symbolism can have both a primary and secondary meaning—one which is clearly identified in the text, and the other which requires an interpretation. One apocalyptic symbol which is used in both the Old and New Testaments is a dragon. The word is mentioned five times in the King James translation of the Old Testament (Neh. 2:13, Psa. 91:13, Isa. 27:1, Isa. 51:9, Jer. 51:34). The Hebrew word used is *tanniyn*. It was used in ancient times to describe a large marine creature or a mythological monster of chaos that was opposed to God. It could describe a whale, a jackal, or a serpent. Isaiah 27:1 describes a seven-headed serpent called leviathan. This seven-headed creature is also alluded to in the imagery in Revelation 12:3-4:

> *"And another sign appeared in heaven: behold, a great, fiery red dragon having seven heads and ten horns, and seven diadems on his heads. His tail drew a third of the stars of heaven and threw them to the earth."*

John explains the meaning of this symbolism, that the dragon is identified as Satan himself. The Greek word for *dragon* is *drakon,* and this is why it is translated as "dragon" in the King James version of the Bible. The word dragon is found thirteen times from Revelation 12:3 to 20:2, and it alludes to a large serpent that has special powers.

From early history, when nations were formed and leaders were chosen, it was common to select an animal that represented the empire or nation. When the American colonies won their independence from Britain, they chose an eagle as their national symbol. A story circulated at that time which claimed that Benjamin Franklin preferred a turkey, arguing that the eagle has bad moral character because it steals food from hawks and is too lazy to fish for itself. The turkey, he said, is a more respectable bird and native to America. Interestingly, the eagle was also the symbol for the ancient Roman Empire.

Globally, China is known to have the symbol of a red dragon. News articles have been written that identify China with a red dragon. They associate the color red with ancient Chinese emperors and also with communism. Throughout history, there hasn't been another nation or empire associated with a color except Red China.

The dragon in Revelation is not just any ordinary dragon, but a *great* dragon. This verse notes the word "great," which in Greek is *megas.* It is the same word used in Revelation 18:18 that describes mystery Babylon as a great city. Since Satan is the primary meaning for the symbol of the dragon (Rev. 12:9), then we must determine how China, the red dragon, might be linked to the great dragon, Satan.

In nations where the leaders and the government are evil, the ordinary people who live under their rule are forced to suffer at the hands of those government leaders. Most Chinese people seem to be reasonable and rational. But the communist leaders, in China and throughout history, have proven themselves to be tyrants who persecute and murder millions of their own citizens. Right now, China has an appalling human rights record, and they seem to work every day to find new ways to oppress their citizens and force compliance and complete obedience to the communist government.

This is the mindset of Satan himself. The actions of the Chinese communist government and their military, along with their satanic alignment, place them in a position to be part of the future beast kingdom at the time of the end.

Whether or not one accepts the double application theory that the great red dragon could be an apocalyptic symbol representing China, we know that Scripture talks about a unified force called the "kings of the East" who will organize a massive military coalition at the time of the end.

## CHAPTER 14

# WHEN GOD CRASHES THE TECH PARTY

Throughout history, some of the mightiest plans of men suddenly have been disrupted by the unexpected intervention of the Almighty. With all the discussions of the wonders of technology, there is a weak link that few tech experts seem to consider. It could bring the entire house of cards crashing down, and it is one way in which the tech party can and prophetically will be disrupted in the future.

The possibility reminds me of the time when King Belshazzar invited his leading politicians to an all-night party at his palace banquet facility that was large enough to hold thousands. The drunken revelry was unexpectedly interrupted by a mysterious hand that wrote a warning on the palace wall. Within twenty-four hours, the empire of Babylon fell to the hands of the Medes and Persians. We have our own "wall," called Wall Street, that posts daily economic activity. At times, America experiences stock crashes after a series of warnings indicate trouble is brewing.

Perhaps the greatest threat to the artificial intelligence chain of technology is the need for electrical power. Even batteries need to be replaced or recharged. Without electricity or some viable and vigorous form of energy, it is virtually impossible to keep phones, computers, televisions, and all forms of communication working.

What are some dangers that would interrupt power and communications, thereby bringing all forms of electronics and artificial intelligence to a standstill? Some of these possibilities have already occurred on a small scale, while we often are warned about others.

## DISRUPTION OF POWER

In the United States, the primary energy sources include:

- natural gas (31.8%)
- petroleum (28%)
- coal (17.8%)
- renewable energy, which includes biomass, geothermal, hydropower, solar, and wind (12.7%)
- nuclear electric power (9.6%)

The American Geosciences Institute says that the five sectors that consume energy are:

- industrial sector, which includes facilities and equipment used for manufacturing, agriculture, mining, and construction (uses 32% of all energy consumption in the U.S.)
- transportation sector, which includes all vehicles that transport people or goods, including everything from cars and motorcycles to trains and ships (uses 29% of all energy consumption in the U.S.)

- residential sector, which covers homes, apartments, and other places where people live (uses 20% of all energy consumption in the U.S.)
- commercial sector, which covers everything that involves use by citizens and consumers, such as malls, restaurants, hospitals, schools, hotels, churches, warehouses, places of public assembly, and so on (uses 18% of all energy consumption in the U.S.)
- electric power section, which uses primary energy to generate most of the electricity consumed by the other sectors.[64]

It is interesting to research the pros and cons of various forms of renewable energy, which are being touted as being among the only forms of energy that will save the planet from humanity. Renewable energy research is beyond the scope of this book, but watch for ongoing stories and discussions about renewable energy. Wind turbines are especially controversial. So is the push for electric cars.

An estimated 62,500 power plants are in operation around the world. Nine of the largest operating power plants are hydroelectric, meaning they use water from some source, such as rivers, dams, or a reservoir. Of those nine, four are in China. Brazil has two, and the United States, Russia, and Venezuela each have one. Japan has one of the ten largest power plants in the world, but theirs is nuclear.[65]

A great amount of water is needed to generate energy through hydroelectricity. It takes the force of falling water to power the turbines, which rotate and spin electromagnets to generate current. Finally, the current enters a transformer where the voltage is increased for long distance transmission over power lines.

One of the pressing questions about hydroelectric energy is that of what happens when there is a drought. In 2022, reports from across the

American West showed that reservoirs were drying up. Lake Mead was at a historic low. There was concern that if levels continued to drop, power would be impacted in several states.

Government is pushing for a switch to solar and wind energy, but these forms of energy production have their own problems. First, they do not generate enough power to run entire cities. Neither will they generate the energy needed to power all the electric vehicles being forced upon the world.

Both solar and wind are weather dependent. Solar needs sun because UV light generates the energy. Rainy or overcast days will affect energy production. It is expensive if you are completely dependent on it since it requires batteries to store any excess energy generated by the panels. Solar has a low sun to energy conversion rate. Manufacture and disposal of solar panels creates harm to the environment, particularly because of the plastic waste. Solar uses a lot of space, and obviously the panels cannot be placed in shady areas. No sun equals no energy, meaning that energy is not being produced at night. Think about how you will charge that electric vehicle after you get home at night, so you'll have enough power to drive your car to work the next morning.

Wind turbines require wind to operate, and some areas are less windy than others. Ocean coastlines generate the most wind, but citizens have banded together to fight the installation of wind turbines along their own coastline towns. Often, these people are supportive of "loud and ugly wind turbines" as long as somebody else has to look at them.

Remote areas often generate more wind, but how is wind energy brought from wind farms to areas that need the energy? Wind turbines also affect wildlife because birds are killed when they fly between the turning blades. And let's not forget that, during a winter storm in Texas in 2021, their wind turbines iced over and froze. If this happens in

Texas, what will happen in the northern regions when a winter storm shows up? Wind turbines have been widely criticized because nobody wants to look at them, and they have been proven to be an unreliable source of sustained energy.

Coal and other sources of natural energy have worked well, but environmentalists and climate change activists are determined to force the world into other forms of energy. The intent of the green energy focus is to eliminate all forms of fossil fuel, including coal and natural gas.

The entire world is dependent upon their own forms of national and local power production. We have observed problems such as hurricanes and tornadoes that weave a destructive path, winter storms that cause power outages, or demands on the electrical grid during intense weather that cause rolling blackouts. Storms, earthquakes, and other natural disasters cycle through every year and cause disruptions somewhere in the world.

## HACKERS AND GRID ATTACKERS

Military experts have been concerned for decades about the age and deterioration of the U.S. power grids, as well as the possibility of hacking by nations or organizations that are not our friends at any given moment.

When the Chinese balloon was shot down after it crossed the entire continental United States in 2023, news circulated that it was a spy balloon that was collecting information on either U.S. military bases or U.S. power plants. I asked a retired military expert why the Chinese would be interested in our power plants. He suggested that if China were to attack Taiwan, they would threaten to attack our power plants, thereby shutting down entire sections of the power grid as a deterrent to our interference in their invasion.

Cybersecurity attacks and threats can come from other countries, criminal gangs, professional hackers, or terrorists. Energy regulators and others say that threats to the power system, whether physical or cyber in nature, are becoming more common and complex. Some federal agencies have warned that future wars may not be fought with missiles from ships, but from cyber terrorists working from a small room on behalf of an unfriendly country or rouge organization. Nobody seems to be able to identify the cyberattackers we already have encountered, although we can be guaranteed that somebody will blame Russia.

The likelihood that cyberattacks will continue and become increasingly more severe is guaranteed. It is up to power plants and the government to beef up security and prevent dangerous breeches.

Ask yourself some questions. If threats and attacks are imminent now, what will happen when all these power systems are run by artificial intelligence through a single national or global system and authority? Will individual citizens or entire countries be blackmailed or held hostage over the energy they desperately need? What about apocalyptic natural disasters, especially those the Apostle John saw? How will they affect power and energy?

## ASTEROIDS ARE COMING

In Luke 21:11, one of the cosmic signs at the time of the end is "fearful sights and great signs from heaven." Mark 13:25 gives a similar warning: *"And the stars of heaven shall fall, and the powers that are in heaven shall be shaken."* Prophetically, this would align with Hebrews 12:26 which reads, *"Yet once more I will shake not the earth only, but also heaven."*

"Stars falling" is an ancient phrase that refers to objects in space such as meteorites or asteroids. Evidence from around the world indicates that asteroids have struck Earth in times past, long before towns and cities were constructed.

In 2013, an asteroid entered the earth's atmosphere above Chelyabinsk, Russia, exploding while still 18.5 miles in the air. The kinetic energy before atmospheric impact was equal to the blast of 400 to 500 kilotons of TNT. The asteroid did not cause direct damage because it exploded above ground, but the shockwave caused by the energy it released injured 1,500 people and damaged 7,200 buildings across six cities. Some witnesses said that they felt intense heat, and the light from the asteroid was briefly brighter than the sun.

In 1908 an asteroid exploded above ground in Tunguska, Russia, knocking down approximately eighty million trees over an 830 square mile area. This explosion has been estimated to be a thousand times more powerful than the explosion of the atomic bomb at Hiroshima.[66]

This is the kind of damage an asteroid or meteorite can do when it explodes above ground. Think of the damage one could do if it directly hit the earth. The Apocalypse predicts one major strike in the future that will impact one third of waters on the planet:

> *"...and there fell a great star from heaven, burning as it were a lamp, and it fell upon the third part of the rivers, and upon the fountains of waters; and the name of the star is called Wormwood: and the third part of the waters became wormwood; and many men died of the waters, because they were made bitter.*
>
> – Rev. 8:10-11 (KJV)

## SOLAR FLARES AND STORMS

In Luke 21, Christ predicted strange cosmic activity. He said there will be signs in the sun, moon, and stars that will cause distress and perplexity among nations of the earth (Luke 21:25). Whatever people see happening in the heavens and upon the earth is so frightening that Christ warned of men's hearts failing them for fear and for looking after those things which are coming on the earth, for the powers of heaven shall be shaken (Luke 21:26).

One such danger could possibly come from solar flares and storms. In June of 2023, news reports were suddenly warning of a possible "internet apocalypse" caused by solar storms.

Solar flares are large eruptions of electromagnetic radiation from the sun, which last from minutes to hours and travel at the speed of light. Solar radiation storms occur when a large-scale magnetic eruption accelerates charged particles in the solar atmosphere to very high velocities. When the protons collide with satellites or humans in space, they can penetrate the object that they collide with and cause damage to electronic circuits or biological DNA. When the protons collide with the atmosphere, they create free electrons. These electrons can absorb high frequency radio waves and make radio communication difficult or impossible.[67]

If a solar storm hits the earth, the radiation and geomagnetic storms can affect power grids, communication systems, internet, satellite operations, and navigation capabilities, according to the National Oceanic and Atmospheric Administration (NOAA).

The government knows that this could impact electronics and power. USA Today reported that NASA created a new computer model that combines artificial intelligence and satellite data that could sound the alarm for dangerous space weather. An international team of researchers has been using artificial intelligence to look for weather-related connections that could wreak havoc on technology. They are using the AI method called "deep learning" to train computers to recognize patterns based on previous examples.[68]

A solar storm hitting the earth and causing a severe long-term effect on so much technology would be a rare event, but the Bible does give us a warning. In the latter part of the Great Tribulation, the sun will experience unusual and severe solar activity that increases heat to an unbearable level, causing men to curse God because of the scorching and unbearable heat (Rev. 16:9).

No matter how hard researchers and governments try, no advanced technology will be able to stop what has already been prophesied in Scripture. No quantum computers, no amount of reduction in greenhouse gas, and no amount of hiding light from the sun will stop what has already been ordained by God to happen.

## THE EFFECT OF AN EMP

EMP stands for electromagnetic pulse, which is a massive burst of electromagnetic energy that could occur naturally from geomagnetic disturbances, or it may occur from the use of a nuclear weapon. The government has been concerned that rouge nations, highly organized terrorist groups, or nations at war could release an EMP device on their enemy. An electromagnetic pulse has the potential to create an interruption to every area of human life because it will affect the power grid, electronic devices, and anything that runs on electronics (such as transportation vehicles, appliances, and heating and air conditioning systems).

A nuclear weapon that is detonated in the upper atmosphere would not necessarily kill humans on the ground or damage buildings. But it would affect power and copper wiring. Think of all the items that contain electronic parts. Our utilities would be impacted, as well as computerized systems in cars, our cell phones, global positioning systems, aircraft, and the harvesting, production, and distribution of food. Anything that involves computerization would be affected.

Some nations have been working to find strategies to help protect against damage and disruption caused by an EMP. If a powerful EMP strike occurred over the central United States, the disruption of all things electrical would create havoc on a scale we've never seen. Reports claim that, within six months, ninety percent of the population would be dead or dying, many having starved to death or become the victims of uncontrollable crime.

That sounds hyperbolic, but the numerous wars that are predicted in Scripture will cause peace to be taken from the earth (Rev. 6:4). Nations will be forced to ration food, as shortages and hyperinflation will result in one loaf of bread costing an entire day's pay (Rev. 6:6).

## SHORTAGES OF ELECTRICITY

In Houston, Texas, I enjoyed lunch and conversation with a man who is one of the leading experts overseeing the electrical power in that area. Our conversation turned to electric powered vehicles. The batteries in these vehicles run a certain number of miles on one charge, and they must be recharged or else the vehicle won't operate. People charge the batteries either at charging stations built specifically for electric cars or at a home that has been equipped with an electric car battery charger. Electric cars plugged into an ordinary household electrical outlet would take too long to charge. The Energy Department says that you will add four to five miles of range for every hour your car is charged in a 110v outlet.

According to the U.S. Census Bureau, the city of Houston has an estimated population of over 2.3 million residents. The Houston metro area, made up of nine counties, had over 7.2 million residents in 2022. As of July 2022, there were about 19,000 electric vehicles in the county and 13,000 registered in the city of Houston.

By 2030, the city wants to transition all light vehicles to electric powered, because the federal government is pressuring states and corporations to reduce carbon emissions by sixty-five percent by that year.

If a large percentage of the population were to purchase electric cars, the first problem would be a lack of available charging stations. The second challenge is the amount of available power to charge these large car batteries. If everybody charged their cars in the summer when demand for air conditioning is at its peak, it would most certainly cause electricity to go out in parts of the city.

I had the same conversation about electric cars with a businessman from Birmingham, Alabama who has been a partner of our ministry for many years. One of the supervisors over Birmingham's electrical utilities expressed to my friend his concern about how a huge rise in use of electric vehicles would impact electrical power availability in Birmingham. He said that if everybody in the subdivision where he lives owned electric vehicles and charged them at the same time, without changes to the power stations, at peak times in the summer, it could cause rolling blackouts in the city.

Last year I was sitting at my desk in our office in Cleveland, Tennessee when the power went out and stayed out long enough that we sent our office staff home. My office doesn't have windows, but I made my way to the next office where I picked up three objects from a windowsill. These are small enough to carry in your hand, and they have a solar panel on top. Sunlight had been charging these solar lights, which have a switch for turning on the light and a socket for charging a phone. I was able to work with no electricity because I had these lights. But obviously, these would not power your house, your appliances, or your electric car in the event of a power blackout.

There are several other problems with electric vehicles, one of which is the seldom addressed issue of human rights violations surrounding cobalt mining. Electric car batteries use cobalt, three-fourths of which is mined under appalling conditions in the Congo using slave and child labor. Reports have revealed that even four-year-olds are forced to work twelve hours a day in cobalt mines for ten-cents per day. China, as we might expect, has cornered the cobalt market.[69]

People who claim to fight for human rights will search endlessly for any perceived violation they can dig up in a western country like the United States. But they never express concern when serious violations occur in places like Africa or China. The difference is that, when the violation helps the globalists reach their goal, they will overlook serious violations and negative environmental impacts. In this case, their goal is zero net carbon emissions, and no person or thing that stands in the way of that matters.

Also not addressed is the limited impact this switch to electric vehicles will have on the climate, which is the alleged reason for demanding these changes. Economist Diana Furchtgott-Roth reported on EpochTV that, if the United States eliminated all fossil fuels completely, it would barely make a difference in the temperature—two-tenths of one degree Celsius in the year 2100.

Government demands are imposing huge costs on consumers and businesses. At the same time the government is attempting to mandate that sixty percent of all cars sold by 2030 be electric, they are also forcing power plants to reduce carbon emissions by ninety percent or else shut down. Furchtgott-Roth expects many power plants to shut down because that will be their only option.

Is the picture becoming clear? If globalists want us to own no vehicles, the first step toward accomplishing this is to force the production of electric vehicles, so you have no choice in the matter. The next step is to force our electric utility companies to shut down. Then what is your plan for transportation? One way or another, the globalist plan is to give us no choice except to walk, ride a bicycle, or move to a fifteen-minute smart city where every citizen will be under their complete control and surveillance. Mission accomplished. It is not and never has been about the climate.

Three predicted and uncontrollable apocalyptic events in Scripture will directly impact electricity and its distribution to the citizens in many nations, causing global disruptions of communications and transportation. Those disasters are earthquakes, volcanoes, and the darkening of the sun.

## THE MEGA QUAKE

The Bible warns that many earthquakes will shake the earth in different places (Matt. 24:7). There is a prediction of one earthquake that is so violent and destructive, the cities of the nations will collapse. The prophecy reads:

> *"...And there was a great earthquake, such as was not since men were upon the earth, so mighty an earthquake, and so great... and the cities of the nations' fell..."*
>
> – Revelation 16:17-19

Every large city in the world is dependent upon electronic technology, especially the internet and high-speed communications. There is a near constant buzz of activity in almost every large city as related to the business world, entertainment, transportation, and other activities. Many cities around the world have been dubbed "the city that never sleeps."

The cities "falling" likely alludes to buildings collapsing or becoming abandoned or condemned. When a city falls, we think it typically means something happened that forced people to abandon property and move to another area. Obviously, a disaster of this magnitude would cause problems with communication and electronics.

This earthquake unleashes widespread repercussions. One aftermath is that "every island fled away (disappeared), and the mountains were not found" (Rev. 16:20). Underwater divers have discovered ruins of ancient civilizations, temples, and small communities that once existed before they were submerged under water. Their destruction was linked to either volcanic eruptions, tsunamis, or severe earthquakes. These civilizations were once coastal regions or small islands. When powerful earthquakes occur, especially in the oceans and seas, the resulting tsunamis that cover the land have the force to permanently change the shape of coastlines.

This mega earthquake mentioned in Revelation will collapse buildings and create tsunamis that destroy islands. The result will be an untold number of deaths, along with destruction of man-made technology.

## THE RING OF FIRE

In the book of Revelation, the Apostle John had an apocalyptic vision that included a mountain burning with fire:

> *"And the second angel sounded, and as it were a great mountain burning with fire was cast into the sea: and the third part of the sea became blood; and the third part of the creatures which were in the sea, and had life, died; and the third part of the ships were destroyed."*
>
> – Revelation 8:8-9 (KJV)

Most scholars would agree that this burning mountain is likely a huge volcano that erupts. Joel 2:30-31 predicts an increase in such activity as a sign of the time of the end. The mountain being cast into the sea indicates it is either an island volcano, or else it is located near the coast of a sea or ocean. When the mountain breaks off into the sea, this would create a fast-moving and powerful tsunami, which would explain the destruction of ships and possibly the death of sea life.

## THE SUN BECOMES DARK

One unusual yet common apocalyptic theme is the sun becoming dark (Isa. 13:10; Joel 2:31; 3:15; Matt. 24:29). From a natural viewpoint, this is possible during a severe volcanic eruption which causes volcanic ash to fill the atmosphere and darken the sky because the sun cannot shine through. The ash can be carried over wide areas of land, where it pollutes water, blocks sunlight, and destroys farming.

In Indonesia in April of 1815, the Mount Tambora volcano erupted, killing between ten thousand and eleven thousand people directly, while between forty-nine thousand and ninety thousand died from famine and disease that followed. The ash dispersed around the world and lowered global temperatures so much that 1816 was known as "the year without a summer." The effects of this volcano were said to have been the worst since the Stone Age.

We also cannot discount the likelihood that the darkening of the sun will be caused by global climate activists who are determined to control the temperature and sunlight. Those who serve the god of climate change believe they are doing the world a favor by blocking sunlight from reaching the earth. The United States has recently been encouraged to spend a hundred million dollars to research technology that cools the planet by blocking sunlight. (You might not want to rush out just yet to invest in solar panels.)

An unexplainable contradiction exists between climate change activists who desire to block sunlight from reaching the earth, and futurists who desire to bring the world into an affordable energy Solar Age. It has been a decades-long desire for fossil fuels to be phased out and for renewable energy to come from sources such as the sun. These two groups have conflicting goals, so they need better coordination to decide whether they want sunlight or don't want sunlight. With current technology, it might be difficult to enter the Solar Age without sunlight.

## TECHNOLOGY DEVELOPERS CAN'T STOP WHAT'S COMING

These cataclysmic events are potentially some of the greatest threats to modern technology. Society today cannot function as we know it without the flow of electrical energy, but unexpected natural and human-created disasters can interrupt any global economy and jeopardize the lives of millions of people.

Despite the zeal of climate activists who fly private jets to global climate conferences where they discuss their plans for reducing carbon emissions, no amount of money is going to prevent these biblical disasters. Despite spending billions of tax dollars to "go green" and save the planet, all the world's currency, gold, and silver combined cannot prevent solar flares, asteroids, volcanic eruptions, earthquakes, or tsunamis. When these disasters culminate at the time of the end, it will also be the handwriting on the wall to show that the most advanced generation in world history cannot successfully harness the power of raw nature. They will also realize that no matter how hard they try, they are not God.

## CHAPTER 15

# AI AND TECHNOLOGY WILL EVENTUALLY FAIL

An ancient unwritten rule is concealed in the example of the first attempt to form a global empire under one ruler, which occurred around four thousand years ago. Following an earth changing worldwide flood, a family of survivors—namely Noah, his wife, their three sons, and the sons' three wives—began the process of repopulating the earth. Eventually, Noah's children and their offspring found a plain in the land of Shinar, also known as ancient southern Mesopotamia, and settled there (Genesis 11:1-2). Cities were eventually built along the Tigris and Euphrates rivers, one of the most historically famous being Babel.

The people in Shinar selected one of their own to be their government ruler. His name was Nimrod, a son of Cush and a grandson of Ham, Noah's son. Many Jewish legends abound about Nimrod. Some say that his name suggests rebellion, indicating that he rebelled against God. The Jewish Targums say that he was a murderer of innocent men, and he demanded that men depart from the religion of Shem (Noah's son) and cleave to the institutes of Nimrod. Other sources believe that Nimrod might have been of the remnant of giants that returned to existence after the flood (Gen. 6:4). The inspired Genesis record indicates he was a "mighty hunter" (Gen. 10:9). Moses recorded that Nimrod built the cities of Babel, Erech, Accad, and Calneh—all in the plains of Shinar (Gen. 10:10).

Nimrod was the first man to become what we might call a dictator. He was the absolute ruler of people living in the plains of Shinar and in his four cities. He had the advantage of no communication barriers, as all the people spoke one language. After settling in the plains of Shinar, they said to one another, *"Come, let us build ourselves a city, and a tower whose top is the heavens; let us make a name for ourselves, lest we be scattered abroad over the face of the whole earth"* (Gen. 11:4).

The deaths of millions of people and animals and the destruction by a deluge of water was a past, yet all too present memory for Noah's descendants. The full purpose of the tower is unknown, but some suggest it was built high and upward so that if God ever sent another flood, those at the top would survive the waters.

We can read the statement of the people of Babel and see that the tower was built for three purposes: to unite under one cause—that of building themselves a towered city; to live in one place and keep from being scattered abroad over the earth; and oddly, to make a name for themselves. Today this might be called "branding." Every corporation that is headquartered in towering city skyscrapers has a financial budget that handles only the branding and marketing of their products and services. Some names are universally known, as a famous company has "made a name for itself."

## THE NAME AND TOWER FAILURE

The following verses reveal the response to Nimrod's plan to become the global leader of a new world order following the flood:

> *"But the Lord came down to see the city and the tower which the sons of men had built. And the Lord said, 'Indeed the people are*

> *one and they all have one language, and this is what they begin to do; now nothing that they propose to do will be withheld from them. Come, let Us go down and there confuse their language, that they may not understand one another's speech.' So the Lord scattered them abroad from there over the face of all the earth, and they ceased building the city."*
>
> – Gen. 11:5-8 (NKJV)

Just as with the Tower of Babel, there is a common belief among technology giants and globalists who control the information highway that, if they can work together and join the cities and all humanity under their global banner, the time will come when there is nothing they cannot accomplish. They also seem to have a desire to make a name for themselves.

With the construction of the Tower of Babel, the united language of the people was suddenly confused, and people could not understand one another. Similarly with technology, computers have a language with a series of ones and zeros, which are programmed to create a code that is designed to perform a specific function. When our ministry transitioned from one computer platform to another, it took weeks to get the kinks out. I was told that the new language doesn't understand the code of the old language. This, too, is the Babel effect.

The latest technological revolution is a quantum computer that will far outperform any digital supercomputer. This new technology will greatly assist with the goal of increasing knowledge and accelerating the transhumanist agenda. Combined with artificial intelligence, these quantum computers are expected to wildly exceed anything that can be accomplished by current technology and certainly anything that can be analyzed by the human brain. Michio Kaku says, "Perhaps one day quantum computers will unravel the secrets of the creation of the universe." [70]

It's understandable that people in these industries are continually searching for the next great leap forward. After all, that is their job. But it sounds eerily similar to the claims made by the people in Babel who wanted to build a tower to heaven.

## DESTRUCTION BY WINDS

In 2023, NASA determined that they could use spacecraft and artificial intelligence to measure solar winds, which would allow them to possibly predict an impending solar storm anywhere on the earth with a thirty-minute advance warning. As mentioned, a significant solar storm could strike the earth and severely impact power grids and other critical infrastructure.

When Nimrod constructed the tower that would reach into heaven, the Bible is silent about how the Tower of Babel was destroyed. But some historical writings go further and say that God sent a great wind and destroyed the tower. Both the *Book of Jubilees* and *The Works of Josephus* mention destruction by a great wind.

Notice the parallels. Nimrod constructed a tower to reach heaven, and God sent a wind to destroy it while He confused their language. Today we have modern scientists fearing that solar winds will destroy communication systems, so they place spacecraft in the heavens to predict and warn of the arrival of destructive winds.

The body of Nimrod long ago returned to dust. It is not likely that any of his bones still exist, but if they do, perhaps they are buried somewhere in the plains of Shinar. The pride that caused Nimrod to build a tower to the heavens and make a name for himself, and the arrogance that caused people to defy the Almighty with the belief that "there is nothing we cannot do" remain today in their earthly descendants.

## APOCALYPTIC WARNINGS

Scientists have discussed for years the possible threat to electronics and communications from electromagnetic attacks, solar flares, power grid hackers, and natural disasters. Any of these things would create failures and disruptions that have the potential to be apocalyptic.

John's vision of future events that are recorded in the book of Revelation speak to the dangers of trouble caused by the sun. Cosmic disaster warnings are found in both the Old and New Testaments.

Christ mentioned that, in the last days before His return, strange cosmic signs would appear. He said:

> *"And there will be signs in the sun, in the moon and in the stars, and on the earth distress of nations, with perplexity...."*
>
> – Luke 21:25 (NKJV)

John detailed the sun's activity when he wrote:

> *"And the fourth angel poured out his bowl on the sun; and power was given to him to scorch men with fire. And men were scorched with great heat, and they blasphemed the name of God who has power over these plagues; and they did not repent and give Him glory."*
>
> – Rev. 16:8-9 (NKJV)

This is followed by the verse:

> *"Then the fifth angel poured out his bowl on the throne [headquarters] of the beast; and his kingdom became full of darkness; and they [people on the earth] gnawed their tongues because of the pain."*
>
> – Rev. 16:10 (NKJV)

> *"A third of the sun was struck, a third of the moon, and a third of the stars, so that a third of them were darkened. A third of the day did not shine, and likewise the night."*
>
> – Rev. 8:12 (NKJV)

This strange darkness is predicted in other prophetic warnings throughout the Old Testament where prophets saw the sun and moon being darkened (Ezek. 32:7-9; Joel 2:31; 3:15). The darkness could be a result of the effects from three apocalyptic references. One is the previously mentioned asteroid called *wormwood*. In Revelation 8:11, which immediately precedes the verse about darkness, a star called wormwood causes a third of the waters to become bitter, and many died.

A second darkness occurs when a section of the earth cracks open, producing a smoke like a great furnace that darkens the sun and air (Rev. 9:1-2).

The third reference is a mountain burning with fire. The ancient prophet Joel noted a last day event that he called "*wonders in the heavens and in the earth: Blood and fire and pillars of smoke. The sun shall be turned into darkness...*" (Joel 2:30-31 NKJV). This has been researched from the Hebrew text and Jewish sources, and it is believed to be a prediction of terrible volcanic eruptions that produce fire (lava) and smoke. The smoke covers the atmosphere and blocks sunlight, which would help fulfill the apocalyptic passages about the darkening of the sun, moon, and stars.

## NOBODY CAN STOP THIS

One thing the world has never been able to stop, except perhaps through prayer and divine supernatural intervention, is natural disasters. Destructive hurricanes, tornados, and strong earthquakes impact man-made structures and electrical power, sometimes for days or weeks. Modern societies depend on their utilities and electrical power for nearly everything. On a wide scale, business and communications are disrupted, while on a personal level, appliances and heating or air conditioning are disrupted. This is why so many people who understand the possibility of disruptions prepare for natural disasters.

Except through repentance and turning from their wicked ways, people also have no control over decisions made by the Almighty when He determines that the moral and spiritual corruption of a city or nation has become so bad that He marks it for judgment. One of the Greek words for God's judgment is *krisis*, and it refers to a judgment or decision, as in the concept of determining the correctness of a matter. Greek tribunals would weigh evidence in favor of or against the accused, then determine either innocence or guilt. We often speak of a *crisis,* in which something or someone is in danger or experiencing extreme difficulty.

Before judgment is enacted, all facts must be presented and reviewed. *God always examines all evidence before visiting in judgment.* This is one reason God sent men in the form of angels to Sodom, before He executed the final judgment. He was reconfirming all evidence that had been compiled against the wicked men (Gen. 18-19).

God heard the cries of strangers in Sodom and saw the iniquity, and He set a judgment of destruction against the city. Abraham knew that his nephew and family were in the city, thus he interceded for God's mercy to save Sodom, if ten righteous were found (Gen. 18). Only four righteous individuals remained in the city, giving God a release from the agreement and permission to unleash justice by bringing complete destruction by fire.

In another example, the Israelites turned from God to idolatry when they made a golden calf and danced before it, claiming that it was the god who brought them out of Egypt (Exodus 32). The Lord told Moses that He planned to destroy the entire nation and rebuild a new one through Moses. To stop this plan, Moses appealed to God, reminding Him of His everlasting covenant made to Abraham, Isaac and Jacob. Moses' covenant appeal motivated God, the Judge, to overturn the death sentence against the entire nation.

Only intercession and repentance can alter a heavenly judicial decision. When Jonah warned the city of Nineveh that destruction was coming in forty days if they did not repent, the entire city humbled itself in sackcloth and began turning to the true God. Nineveh was spared.

However, later generations eventually returned to a life of iniquity, and there were no prophetic warnings and no leaders interested in repenting and changing their religion to serve some Hebrew deity. One hundred fifty years after repenting, Nineveh was invaded and destroyed.

In some instances, a divine judgment can be delayed. But if belligerence, unbelief, and spiritual decline persist, the crisis will come to a head. Isaiah asked those in Judea, *"Why should you be stricken again? You will revolt more and more. The whole head is sick…from the sole of the foot even to the head, there is no soundness in it…"* (Isa. 1:5-6 NKJV). When the head (leaders) are sick (corrupt), then the corruption in the head flows to the entire body (nation).

End time events written in Scripture will happen as prophesied by men such as Daniel and the Apostle John. But until that time, it is imperative that people repent and turn from their evil ways, so that divine judgment can be delayed.

## RUNNING WITH KNOWLEDGE

Daniel chapter 12 carries the reader into the time known as the Great Tribulation. Daniel said, *"…there shall be a time of trouble, such as never was since there was a nation, even to that same time…"* He was told to seal up his book (referring to the understanding of what he had written) until the time of the end. At the time of the end, *"many will run to and fro, and knowledge shall be increased"* (Dan. 12:4 KJV). One translation says, *"Many will go back and forth, and knowledge will be increased"* (NASB). The Complete Jewish Bible translates it as, *"Many will rush here and there as knowledge increases."* There are three obvious components in this prediction.

First, the events referred to will take place at the time of the end. Second, "running to and fro" is a phrase that indicates advanced travel ability, something that has only existed in modern times. The third component is knowledge.

Eight different Hebrew words are used for *knowledge* in the Old Testament. In Daniel 12:4, the Hebrew word is *da'ath*, which is the same Hebrew word used for the tree of knowledge of good and evil that was in the Garden of Eden (Gen. 2:9).

Our knowledge today is not gained just by experience or by learning in a classroom or reading a book. Our knowledge is often gained by what we read, hear, and see through the internet or on television. The word for increased in the verse is the Hebrew *rabah*, which means "multiply exceedingly" or "abundantly increase."

Today it isn't just human intelligence that is increasing; it is machine intelligence. When we read about artificial intelligence, we clearly understand how this gives new meaning to "multiply exceedingly" or "abundantly increase." Add quantum computing, and all boundaries are removed.

In the year 1900, human knowledge doubled around every one hundred years. By 1945, human knowledge doubled every twenty-five years. Now we are told that, with the internet, human knowledge is doubling every thirteen months. As unimaginable as this seems, we are told that we can expect to see human knowledge double every twelve hours.[71]

With increased knowledge comes a plea from some people for the First Amendment to be removed from the Constitution, and for the government to control information. The excuse is: How will people know what they're supposed to believe unless the government tells them?

Name one government on the planet, outside the Kingdom of God, that can be trusted with the power to define truth and control information. This leads us back to chapter one and the warning Jesus gave about end time *deception*.

We don't need governments, controlled organizations, news networks, or strangers on social media to tell us what to believe. We need the Holy Spirit, the Spirit of truth, who will guide us to all truth and tell us what the Father is saying (John 16:13). That should be the prayer of every believer, that the Holy Spirit will guide us to all truth and not let us become deceived.

As much as people think technology can be godlike, or create humans who are like God, or create control mechanisms for people who think they are God, the Bible clearly shows us that eventually all this will fail. It reminds me of one of my new favorite songs: "God Made It Fail." Everything the devil tried, God made it fail.

Men attempted similar things throughout history, albeit on a much smaller scale because they didn't have the technology. Despite limitless knowledge, unlimited technology, and unlimited ability to collect data and draw conclusions, man's attempts will fail. They will fail through natural disasters and the evils of humanity. They will fail when Jesus returns to rule on Earth for a thousand years. The elitists, the technocrats, the mega corporations, and the governments of the world can sink their last dime into the development of godlike technology, but one day it's all going to fail.

Humanity will never create eternal life in a utopian environment. Only through a redemptive covenant with Jesus Christ can we have eternal life in a perfect environment. Without being born again, people aren't going to like their final eternal destination, which might be why they want to avoid death at all costs. If an atheist can find a way to live forever, he thinks he won't have to worry about the hereafter. This, of course, is another great deception.

Medical breakthroughs, medicines, and technological devices can help prolong lives. But as Paul told us, the outward man (the body) is perishing, while the inward man (the spirit) is renewed day by day (2 Cor. 4:16). We don't reengineer our brains; we renew our minds and spirits.

If you want eternal life in a place that exceeds the imagination or creative abilities of humanity and machines, you have that promise through a covenant of redemption, which is provided through the death and resurrection of the Messiah, Jesus Christ.

## THE FULLNESS OF TIME

When Old Testament prophets predicted the appearance of a King-Messiah, hundreds and sometimes thousands of years passed before the world saw the fulfillment. "*When the fullness of time had come, God sent forth His Son, born of a woman*" (Gal. 4:4).

The New Testament speaks of another coming age called the *fullness of times* when "*He might gather together in one all things in Christ, both which are in heaven and which are on earth—in Him*" (Eph. 1:10). This event, the *gathering together to Him* (2 Thess. 2:1), is also called the Rapture—a word used to describe the catching away of the living saints to Heaven (1 Thess. 4:13-17).

The fullness of time is marked by certain signs, called the *signs of the times* (Matt. 16:3) or the *time of the end* (Dan. 12:4, 9). One significant sign of the time of the end is that "*many will run to and fro, and knowledge will increase*" (Dan. 12:4). The book of Revelation speaks of a cashless form of economic activity, as well as the creation of a talking and living image that will deceive the masses and gather a religious following, under the supervision of a religious false prophet (Rev. 13).

The technological advances made by those who seek to become like God indicate that artificial intelligence will play a role in fulfilling significant biblical prophecies. In the fullness of time, prophetic events will come to pass, and there will be no stopping them.

One day, all this is coming. And so is the return of our Messiah!

The Old Testament prophets searched diligently for the first appearance of the Messiah (1 Peter 1:10). Likewise, our generation of alert believers will continue to search Scriptures and discern the times and warnings, as we watch for the blessed hope—the return of our Lord and Savior Jesus Christ.

Just like Babel's famed tower, the god of AI will fall. In the end, Christ wins.

# NOTES

## Chapter 1: A Two-Thousand-Year-Old Warning


1 "What is artificial intelligence?" IBM, accessed August 16, 2023, https://www.ibm.com/topics/artificial-intelligence.

2 Elizabeth Napolitano, "AI eliminated nearly 4,000 jobs in May, report says," *CBS News*, June 2, 2023, https://www.cbsnews.com/news/ai-job-losses-artificial-intelligence-challenger-report/.

3 OpenAI, "Introducing ChatGPT," accessed August 16, 2023, https://openai.com/blog/chatgpt.

4 Alex Swoyer, "AI could face lawsuits over defamation, product liability, scholars warn," *Washington Times,* April 13, 2023, https://www.washingtontimes.com/news/2023/apr/13/ai-could-face-lawsuits-over-defamation-product-lia/.

5 Shannon Thaler, "ChatGPT 'hallucination' falsely said radio host embezzled money, suit says," *New York Post*, June 7, 2023, https://nypost.com/2023/06/07/mark-walters-suing-chatgpt-for-embezzled-hallucination/.

6 Victor Tangermann, "Google staff warned its AI was a 'pathological liar' before they released it anyway," Futurism, April 19, 2023, https://futurism.com/the-byte/google-staff-warned-ai-pathological-liar.

7 Ben Wodecki, "Samsung to fire employees caught using ChatGPT," *AI Business*, May 2, 2023, https://aibusiness.com/nlp/samsung-to-fire-employees-caught-using-chatgpt.

8 Breck Dumas, "OpenAI forces shutdown of conservative ChatGPT-powered AI bot, creator claims," *Fox Business*, June 7, 2023, https://www.foxbusiness.com/technology/openai-forces-shutdown-conservative-chatgpt-powered-ai-bot-creator-claims.

9 Sejal Sharma, "Stanford researchers claim ChatGPT's performance and accuracy has decreased over time," Interesting Engineering, July 20, 2023, https://interestingengineering.com/science/chatgpts-performance-and-accuracy-has-decreased-over-time-stanford-research.

10 Maggie Harrison, "AI loses its mind after being trained on AI-generated data," Futurism, July 12, 2023, https://futurism.com/ai-trained-ai-generated-data.

11 Klaus Schwab, "The Fourth Industrial Revolution," World Economic Forum, accessed August 16, 2023, https://www.weforum.org/about/the-fourth-industrial-revolution-by-klaus-schwab.

12 "What is the Fourth Industrial Revolution?" World Economic Forum, accessed August 16, 2023, https://www.youtube.com/watch?v=kpW9JcWxKq0.

**Chapter 2: Scammers, Liars, and a Crisis of False Images**

13 Ben Cost, "AI clones teen girl's voice in $1M kidnapping scam: 'I've got your daughter,'" *New York Post,* April 12, 2023, https://nypost.com/2023/04/12/ai-clones-teen-girls-voice-in-1m-kidnapping-scam/.

14 Ben Cost, "AI clones teen girl's voice in $1M kidnapping scam: 'I've got your daughter,'" *New York Post*, April 12, 2023, https://nypost.com/2023/04/12/ai-clones-teen-girls-voice-in-1m-kidnapping-scam/.

15 Austin Westfall, "AI voice-cloning scams are on the rise—here's how you can protect yourself," *Fox Business*, June 8, 2023, https://www.foxbusiness.com/technology/ai-voice-cloning-scams-rise-heres-how-protect-yourself.

16 "Malicious Actors Manipulating Photos and Videos to Create Explicit Content and Sextortion Schemes," Federal Bureau of Investigation, Public Service Announcement, Alert Number I-060523-PSA, June 5, 2023, https://www.ic3.gov/Media/Y2023/PSA230605.

17 "Caller ID Spoofing," Federal Communications Commission, accessed August 16, 2023, https://www.fcc.gov/spoofing.

**Chapter 3: The Spirit Behind AI**

18 Alex Mitchell, "Goodbye privacy: AI's next terrifying advancement is reading your mind," *New York Post*, May 2, 2023, https://nypost.com/2023/05/02/ais-next-terrifying-advancement-is-reading-your-mind/.

19 Julia Mueller, "Musk: There's a chance AI 'goes wrong and destroys humanity,'" *The Hill*, May 17, 2023, https://thehill.com/policy/technology/4008144-musk-theres-a-chance-ai-goes-wrong-and-destroys-humanity/.

20 Julia Mueller, "Musk: There's a chance AI 'goes wrong and destroys humanity,'" *The Hill*, May 17, 2023, https://thehill.com/policy/technology/4008144-musk-theres-a-chance-ai-goes-wrong-and-destroys-humanity/.

21 Julia Mueller, "Musk: There's a chance AI 'goes wrong and destroys humanity,'" *The Hill*, May 17, 2023, https://thehill.com/policy/technology/4008144-musk-theres-a-chance-ai-goes-wrong-and-destroys-humanity/.

22 "An Overview of Catastrophic AI Risks," Center for AI Safety, accessed August 16, 2023, https://www.safe.ai/ai-risk.

**Chapter 4: Transhumanists: The God Makers**

23 "Professor Yuval Harari—How technology will turn men into gods," The Artificial Intelligence Channel, accessed August 16, 2023, https://www.youtube.com/watch?v=FzitBZApt0Q.

24 "What is neural lace?" Global Manufacturing and Industrialization Summit, accessed August 16, 2023, https://gmisummit.com/pdfs/what-is-neural-lace-1.pdf.

25 Yuval Noah Harari, "The Discovery of Ignorance, excerpt from chapter 14, *Sapiens, A Brief History of Humankind*," https://www.ynharari.com/topic/future/.

26 Giovanni Tiso, "Artificial intelligence and the dream of eternal life," Wellcome Collection, March 11, 2019, https://wellcomecollection.org/articles/XH-7QBAAAFlDH0xf.

27 Sharon Gaudin, "Total recall: Storing every life memory in a surrogate brain," Computerworld, April 2, 2008, https://www.computerworld.com/article/2536328/total-recall--storing-every-life-memory-in-a-surrogate-brain.html.

28 Mike Elgan, "Lifelogging is dead (for now)," Computerworld, April 4, 2016, https://www.computerworld.com/article/3048497/lifelogging-is-dead-for-now.html.

29 Michio Kaku. *Quantum Supremacy* [New York: Doubleday, 2023], 3

30 Tom Hartsfield, "Horror stories of cryonics: The gruesome fates of futurists hoping for immortality," Big Think, August 3, 2022, https://bigthink.com/the-future/cryonics-horror-stories/.

**Chapter 5: DNA Manipulation: Creating Demigods**

31 "Why humanized mice?" The Jackson Laboratory, July 21, 2020, https://www.jax.org/news-and-insights/jax-blog/2020/july/why-humanized-mice.

32 "Cloning Fact Sheet," NIH National Human Genome Research Institute, last updated August 15, 2020, https://www.genome.gov/about-genomics/fact-sheets/Cloning-Fact-Sheet.

33 "Cloning Summary," NIH National Library of Medicine: Medline Plus, accessed August 16, 2021, https://medlineplus.gov/cloning.html.

34 "Genetic Engineering," NIH National Human Genome Research Institute, updated August 16, 2023, https://www.genome.gov/genetics-glossary/Genetic-Engineering.

35 "Human Genome Editing Overview," World Health Organization, accessed August 16, 2023, https://www.who.int/health-topics/human-genome-editing#tab=tab_1

36 Katherine J. Wu, "Crispr gene editing can cause unwanted changes in human embryos, study finds," *New York Times*, October 31, 2020, https://www.nytimes.com/2020/10/31/health/crispr-genetics-embryos.html#:~:text=A%20powerful%20gene%2Dediting%20tool,a%20new%20study%20has%20found.

37 Katherine J. Wu, "Crispr gene editing can cause unwanted changes in human embryos, study finds," *New York Times*, October 31, 2020, https://www.nytimes.com/2020/10/31/health/crispr-genetics-embryos.html#:~:text=A%20powerful%20gene%2Dediting%20tool,a%20new%20study%20has%20found.

38 Leah Eisenstadt, "Researchers uncover a new CRISPR-like system in animals that can edit the human genome," *MIT News*, June 28, 2023, https://news.mit.edu/2023/fanzor-system-in-animals-can-edit-human-genome-0628.

39 Justin Martyr, "How the Angels Transgressed," Second Apology, Chapter 5.

**Chapter 6: Robots in Your Future**

40 Alex Shashkevich, "Stanford researcher examines earliest concepts of artificial intelligence, robots in ancient myths," *Stanford News*, February 28, 2019, https://news.stanford.edu/2019/02/28/ancient-myths-reveal-early-fantasies-artificial-life/.

41 "AI robots admit they'd run earth better than 'clouded' humans," *Science Magazine*, July 11, 2023, https://www.thesciencemag.com/2023/07/ai-robots-admit-theyd-run-earth-better.html

42 James Lambert and Edward Cone, "How robots change the world," Oxford Economics, June 26, 2019, https://www.oxfordeconomics.com/resource/how-robots-change-the-world/.

43 Sam Daley, "Robotics: What are robots? Robotics definition and uses," Built In, August 18, 2022 https://builtin.com/robotics.

44 Sam Daley, "Robotics: What are robots? Robotics definition and uses," Built In, August 18, 2022 https://builtin.com/robotics.

45 Carlo Ratti and Richard Florida, "The 15-minute city meets human needs but leaves desires wanting. Here's why," World Economic Forum, November 15, 2021, https://www.weforum.org/agenda/2021/11/15minute-city-falls-short/.

46 "King of Bahrain lands in Dubai with his robot bodyguard," accessed August 16, 2023 "https://www.youtube.com/watch?v=ljwWLMos94Q."

47 "Boston Dynamics' new robot makes soldiers obsolete, here's why," accessed August 16, 2023, https://www.youtube.com/watch?v=Wu1kpnCylKQ.

**Chapter 7: Humans Still Want to be Like God**

48 "Professor Yuval Harari—How technology will turn men into gods," The Artificial Intelligence Channel, accessed August 16, 2023, https://www.youtube.com/watch?v=FzitBZApt0Q.

49 "Professor Yuval Harari—How technology will turn men into gods," The Artificial Intelligence Channel, accessed August 16, 2023, https://www.youtube.com/watch?v=FzitBZApt0Q.

50 Yuval Harari, "New religions of the 21st century," Talks at Google, accessed August 16, 2023, https://www.youtube.com/watch?v=g6BK5Q_Dblo.

51 "Professor Yuval Harari—How technology will turn men into gods," The Artificial Intelligence Channel, accessed August 16, 2023, https://www.youtube.com/watch?v=FzitBZApt0Q.

52 TOI Staff, "Yuval Noah Harari warns AI can create religious texts, may inspire new cults," The Times of Israel, May 3, 2023, https://www.timesofisrael.com/yuval-noah-harari-warns-ai-can-create-religious-texts-may-inspire-new-cults/.

53 “Elon Musk tells Tucker potential dangers of hyper-intelligent AI,” *Fox News*, https://www.youtube.com/watch?v=a2ZBEC16yH4.

**Chapter 9: Crypto and Digital Global Currency**

54 Pei Li, “China’s Social Credit System,” Prager U, April 25, 2022, https://www.prageru.com/video/chinas-social-credit-system?gclid=EAIaIQobChMIkvHvkK76_wIVPEZ_AB0ECQvkEAMYASAAEgK7svD_BwE.

**Chapter 10: Older Citizens in an AI World**

55 Yuval Noah Harari, “How to survive the 21st century,” Betazone Davos 2020, World Economic Forum, accessed August 16, 2023, https://www.youtube.com/watch?v=Rw9FSYH6kL8.

**Chapter 11: End-Time Technology Prophecies**

56 “Amazon One palm payment technology is coming to all 500+ Whole Foods Market stores in the U.S.,” July 30, 2023, https://www.aboutamazon.com/news/retail/amazon-one-whole-foods-market-palm-scanning.

57 Katherine Latham, “The microchip implants that let you pay with your hand,” *BBC News*, April 11, 2022, https://www.bbc.com/news/business-61008730.

**Chapter 12: Is the Image of the Beast AI?**

58 TOI Staff, "Yuval Noah Harari warns AI can create religious texts, may inspire new cults," *The Time of Israel*, May 3, 2023, https://www.timesofisrael.com/yuval-noah-harari-warns-ai-can-create-religious-texts-may-inspire-new-cults/.

59 "Protestants attend AI-led church service in Germany," accessed August 16, 2023, https://www.youtube.com/watch?v=8P9oSgrT35o.

60 "Definition of avatar," Merriam-Webster Dictionary, https://www.merriam-webster.com/dictionary/avatar.

**Chapter 13: Will Mystery Babylon Be a Smart City?**

61 John Foxe. *The New Foxe's Book of Martyrs* [Florida: Bridge-Logos Publishers, 2001], 12-13.

62 "This is NEOM," accessed August 16, 2023, https://www.youtube.com/watch?v=z2Fy4e-ZUb8.

62 "What is Neom?", accessed August 16, 2023, https://www.Neom.com.

63 "The Line | The City of the Future," accessed August 16, 2023, https://www.youtube.com/watch?v=eoDR8wgoCM8.

63 "What is the Line?" accessed August 16, 2023, https://www.youtube.com/watch?v=0kz5vEqdaSc.

**Chapter 14: When God Crashes the Tech Party**

64 "What are the major sources and users of energy in the United States?" American Geosciences Institute, accessed August 16, 2023, https://www.americangeosciences.org/critical-issues/faq/what-are-major-sources-and-users-energy-united-states.

65 "The world's nine largest operating power plants are hydroelectric facilities," U.S. Energy Information Administration, October 18, 2016, https://www.eia.gov/todayinenergy/detail.php?id=28392.

66 "Notable Asteroid Impacts in Earth's History," The Planetary Society, accessed August 16, 2023, https://www.planetary.org/notable-asteroid-impacts-in-earths-history.

67 "Solar radiation storm," The Space Weather Prediction Center, accessed August 16, 2023, https://www.swpc.noaa.gov/phenomena/solar-radiation-storm.

68 Eric Lagatta, "Internet apocalypse: How NASA's solar-storm studies could help save the web," *USA Today,* June 28, 2023, https://www.usatoday.com/story/news/nation/2023/06/28/nasa-internet-apocalypse-solar-storm-prep/70361827007/.

69 Meredith Wolf Schizer, "Clean Energy's Dirty Secret—Human Rights Abuses in Cobalt Mining," *Newsweek Magazine*, January 25, 2023 by Meredith Wolf Schizer https://www.newsweek.com/2023/02/10/clean-energys-dirty-secrethuman-rights-abuses-cobalt-mining-1775174.html.

**Chapter 15: AI and Technology Will Eventually Fail**

70 Michio Kaku. *Quantum Supremacy* [New York: Doubleday, 2023], 3-7

71 "How fast is knowledge doubling?" Lodestar Solutions, accessed August 16, 2023, https://lodestarsolutions.com/keeping-up-with-the-surge-of-information-and-human-knowledge/.